Beyond Myself

Beyond Myself

Release From Despair

Lissa Shortt

Marshall Pickering

Marshall Morgan & Scott
Marshall Pickering
3 Beggarwood Lane, Basingstoke, Hants, RG23 7LP, UK

First published 1986 by Marshall Morgan & Scott Publications Ltd
Part of the Marshall Pickering Holdings Group
A subsidiary of the Zondervan Corporation

ISBN 0 551 01345 1

Typeset in Times Roman by Brian Robinson, North Marston, Bucks
Printed in Great Britain by Hazell Watson & Viney Ltd, Member of the BPCC Group, Aylesbury, Bucks.

For Mike

Acknowledgements

I am grateful to Lucinda and William, Kate and James for the time they have permitted me to work on this book! It has not only made our times together all the more treasured – for me the present has more meaning because I have come to terms with the past.

Not one word would have been written without the encouragement of Edward England nor should I have persevered had I not been able to rely on several kind friends and Kath, Nannie, Beverley and Selina, George and Lydia, who at different times filled in with the children when I could not – I want them to know what that has meant to me.

Dear Gill Brentford read the first draft which was enormously helpful, provoking me to some gritty soul-searching. Frances Tulloch's support gave me confidence and I found in Isabel Murray a rare and excellent critical eye which helped me when I was struggling to finish.

But, most of all, I am especially grateful to Mike, my husband, who has been patient and wise over many years – and has generously allowed me to go to print.

Contents

Foreword

This story incorporates so many diverse strands that it was not immediately clear to me that they could be collected into one book. But I became convinced, as much by the very amorphous collection of material as anything else, that this was a coherent whole. The determining factor was the level beneath what seemed to be happening, namely, what God was doing.

Chapter 1

All for nothing

Still glowing from a hot bath, I put my book down, rolled on to my side and switched the light off. It was early but I was already enjoying the beckoning of sleep. Pregnancy had relaxed me – that marvellous sense of achievement without having to do anything.

A steady drift away from consciousness was interrupted by the baby's physical jerks. I put a hand on my stomach exploring the extent of the protrusion. The movements stopped, then began again. No longer gentle. I straightened upon to my back, placing a hand on each side of the baby, carefully, as though it were fragile. Soothing it, and yet savouring the experience. This hadn't happened before.

And then I whispered, 'You are feeling energetic, little one! If you are going to be this active, I shall get no sleep at all from now on.' The fluttering made me intensely excited. This experience of vigorous life was thrilling.

Then the movements became phrenetic. For a minute at least there was an almighty tumbling. I could feel the hardness of bony elbows and tiny feet. The baby was thrashing around with a vengeance, the activity a contrast to my stillness as I lay in the darkness . . . waiting. Then the movements stopped.

I must have been crazy! That I lay there . . . hopeful, was the madness.

The ultra-sound probe passed back and forth across my greasy stomach. I stared into the monitoring screen. The picture told me nothing. I could see my baby: two arms, two legs and a head. And it was moving. Or was that a visual effect of the scanner? It was momentarily reassuring. Even the brusqueness of the woman operating the machine instilled confidence. Hadn't I been told that she really knew what she was doing? The consultant at Guy's had said:

'We are sending you down to Lewisham. The doctor there is exceptionally good with these machines. We are not getting anywhere here, are we?'

The previous day had been a torture of uncertainty. But the failure to identify a positive foetal heartbeat seemed less threatening with this new doctor and the clear visual impression on the screen. I was being optimistic for as long as I could.

For several more minutes I looked on, feeling at a considerable disadvantage. Prostrate on the bed, my belly exposed, and very short of breath. Eventually I managed to ask my question: 'Can you tell me . . . because I can see the outline of my baby . . . the baby isn't dead – is it?'

Her reply was immediate, without thinking. 'Of course it's dead. It's got a hole in its head.'

I could feel a thud in my forehead. As though my heart had stopped circulating the blood up there. Then a peculiar nausea hit me – I was in agony. I began screaming. And no one was going to touch me, or come near me.

Someone may have put an arm out to steady me as I got off the bed and was led to the changing cubicle. But it was as if life itself had left me. God knew, I felt so utterly apart from my surroundings. So alone and so empty. Completely unprepared for this devastation. As I removed the hospital gown I went on crying, the tears distorting my vision. No wonder the baby hadn't grown as much as I would have expected. I rubbed my hand round it. Gently caressing.

'My baby, my baby – I've talked to you, loved and longed for you and this woman says, 'It's got a hole in *its* head'. You can feel this trauma of emotion within me, can't you? You can feel me, this hand . . . I can touch you. You can't be dead . . . we are together. You can't have gone. What'll I do with this love I have inside me? It'll well up without destination.'

I had to wait for it to sink in . . . my baby is *dead*.

I slipped on my dress, my arms heavy as I dragged the zip up my back. Wiping at my tears with my sleeve, I couldn't believe that I had not faced the situation until this moment. With so many negative results in Guy's yesterday, how could I have been so thick? My optimism had been a shield, a protection against facing the truth. Or perhaps a means of reserving strength for when the bomb dropped.

It is peculiar the disjointed thoughts that go through one's mind at such moments. Elvis Presley's dead too, I reflected as we wound our way through the dingy hospital corridors towards the car park. The nurse and I climbed the two steps up into the mini-bus. I stared out at the dull August day, as we made our slow journey north. South London was not only awash with lively, living shoppers, but some of them were actually laughing. It seemed impossible that they weren't feeling what

I was experiencing – I hurt so much, it must surely have pervaded the air. Hopelessness was creeping in, and I was frightened.

The shock was not easily absorbed. I swung between the image I had evolved of the long-anticipated, soft-skinned bundle, and the miserable truth. That truth was one second like the cutting of a surgeon's knife, going deeper, and the next it left me numb, without any recognisable feeling. My heart and head were on a merry-go-round . . . and the painted horses had bolted. The nurse was no help. She seemed embarrassed, poor girl. I talked to her to help myself to be rational, to attempt to put brakes on my reeling thoughts. But she did not know what 'they' would do next. That would at least have anchored my apprehension about the rest of the day.

The thought, 'I have carried this baby for twenty-seven weeks . . . for nothing' went round and round in my mind.

Back on the ward in Guy's, I stood limply by the window staring out over the roofs. So many roofs, so many people under them, all with their own experience of tragedy – some infinitely worse than mine – and beyond, the river, looking like my spirits felt, grey and muddy. A trolley phone was wheeled in and I dialled Mike's number at work.

When he came on the line I paused, hoping for the right words. 'It's the worst,' I told him. 'I have not yet been told what will happen next, but the baby is dead. It's something to do with the four quarters of the skull . . . they haven't joined, and there's a huge hole. Oh, the way the woman said it! I thought I was going to fall apart. I can't begin to describe how ghastly it was. I'm in a bad way . . .'

'Look, I can't talk like this on the phone and I want to be with you,' he interrupted. 'Hang on, it'll only take me a quarter of an hour to get across the river.' As I hung up the doctor came in. 'We want to get you started as soon as possible. Is your husband here?'

'Not yet, but I have just been speaking to him, he's coming now. What are you going to do? I think I'm going to be your problem. I feel quite hopeless.'

Ignoring my last comment he simply answered the question. 'We shall put up a drip. You should go into labour pretty quickly. Have you heard of epidural anaesthesia? With that there will be no pain, which in the circumstances is the least we can do. Do you want to ask me anything else?'

His tone had become informal, speaking more as the friend he now was. I couldn't ask anything else because I could not bear to hear more. I took in what little he had said and watched him and the nurse leave the room, clearly saving discussion for when I was out of earshot.

So I was on my own when Mike walked in. We hugged and cried a bit together. Then he had a good howl. Two o'clock came and went. At ten past I was taken into the delivery room. People arrived, some in green, others in white, all wearing white shoes or clogs. Unhappily, I was the centre of attention.

My natural inclination to be positive went against the advice I was being given. 'Have a cry, dear – go on!' But how could I in front of them all? Besides, I froze in fear when I saw the needle for the drip. I had my work cut out in trying not to faint!

Then there was the waiting. It was punctuated only by adjustments to the way I was lying, and Mike's welcome support. He tried to encourage me, his face belying the reassurance of his words, and circumstances conspiring to make us separately and variably miserable. He had to watch while I suffered in a drama in which he could play no real part.

At about five o'clock I got the shakes, which overtook me, till someone found a huge piece of 'cooking foil', an arctic blanket I think it was called. This was laid over the five ordinary blankets. Finally, 'oven ready', my epidural topped up, the chattering teeth abated and I drifted into sleep.

The clock showed 2.00 am when I awoke properly. It was so quiet. The activity, of which I had been only slightly aware, was past. Now it was just me and the nursing sister, and the job on hand. The hours that had passed since the epidural catheter had scrunched into my spine had eased the acute fear. Now I felt drowsy but comfy – except for one thing. Anxiety that I might have missed the actual event.

'Nurse, I haven't had the baby, have I?' The possibility was alarming.

'No, nothing happened while you slept.' There was kindness in her voice. She seemed more like a friend I had known for years than someone I had only glimpsed before now in the ante-natal clinic.

I tried to express myself more freely. The only words which came, over and over, were, 'I am sorry'. And God knows, I was. Sorry about everything. About taking up hospital time and a room . . . that I was there at all . . . and there would be nothing at the end of it. And then I felt the need to push.

The sister switched on a brilliant Anglepoise light. I could read her face before she spoke, and there was neither excitement nor expectancy in her tone. 'I can see the head, it's coming now. Can you push hard when I tell you to? It's nearly over. Now . . . good girl. Push now . . . go on p-u-sh. And again . . .!'

I couldn't feel any pain. But the baby's head seemed like a soft, soapy ball. I had an extraordinary sense of the history of the moment. I had not expected to get pregnant. If it never happened again, I would at least now know what people meant when they spoke of the second stage of labour. For that I felt profoundly grateful and entered into my role from the depths of my soul.

'Go on, Lissa! You've nearly done it. Really push as hard as you can.'

There was a sensation of slipperiness and then I felt the baby brush against my inner thigh, . . . 'Oh God . . . no . . . No, no, no. Oh, no . . .!' My baby was being taken away from me, into a side room. I ached for that child. I yearned to feel it – the physical loss intolerable. (Because the baby had died two weeks earlier apparently the child was too disfigured for me to see.)

Sister came back into the room to take my hand in hers and reassure me. 'Lissa, it is a blessing the baby died, believe me. It is terrible for you, but she could not have lived.' She looked me square in the eyes and went on, 'You have been a good girl. Well done. I'll try and find you a cup of tea before I wheel you along to your room.' When she reached the door, she paused and looked back. 'I am sorry,' she said. I was practically asleep by the time I was lifted, washed and on to a bed for the night.

From my room I heard no babies. The next day brought more dull skies and two sensitive visitors. It was quiet and uneventful except for the sinking feeling I had when Mike began describing the telephone conversation he had had with my mother . . . a sad disaster born out of their shock and anxiety. Mike had hung up.

I had the company of the nurses and a certain aura of safeness with which the hospital surrounded me. But I was helpless and incapable of giving anything to Mike. As he left I could hardly bear to think of him returning again to an empty house.

That night was strange. Fitful sleep punctuated by intense mental activity. I was thankful to be alone and just kept going over and over everything that had happened. My brain longed to be able to slot things into place. To know the security of co-ordinating why, and what next, and how to cope. But there was none.

Only days ago we had been walking in Scotland feasting our eyes upon the Cuillins and now this.

As dawn rose I felt not rested, but much calmer. My baby's existence had become real to me. She was now in another world, but she had been known and loved while I had carried her.

During the hours of darkness I had found my comfort. I could now see the significance of that night which I believed was the time of her death. I indulged myself by reliving that particular sensation of fluttering and jerking movements so many times, that I began to be once again transported into the event. Remembering them gave me a special place to focus on. Her life had become no longer supportable. In that moment, in the face of her severe malformation, the struggle to maintain existence was over. As her nerves screamed, the impulses seemed to reach beyond her body and through mine. She had been telling me that something cataclysmic was happening.

It was impossible to forget.

Chapter 2

The real thing

Standing in front of the curtainless window, I stared across the Umbrian plains. I was twenty years old and had been spending two perfect months in Perugia, with my friend Rosie.

The landscape was very still. It gave one the feeling that one was eavesdropping – just as I always felt when I walked the dog after dinner on the farm in Dorset. This was 7 am but I'd been awake for several hours, since the sun first filtered shyly across the countryside. I had lain there staring at the sky. Now I was fully awake and more receptive to the flood of memories that were crowding in on me. Tomorrow I should be gone. Away from the university, a handful of good friends and long chaotic lunches in isolated farmhouses.

The following day I slumped in my seat in the railway carriage more apprehensive about this next stage of the journey than I had ever been about our joint venture in Perugia. Rosie had left that morning for England. The next month was full of uncertainties. The most pressing being the impending arrival of someone with whom I had agreed to spend a week's holiday on Elba. We had discussed the idea months before, but now I was beginning to get cold feet!

Our relationship, that had only just begun when I had set out for Italy, had deepened. I can't say unexpectedly – though perhaps alarmingly! I had not anticipated getting this involved, finding a special person, while I was still so young. He, nearly eight years my senior, felt none of this.

So we had corresponded and our emotional understanding of each other grew as we wrote about the experiences which had been significant in the development of our ideas.

Whilst one side of me was cautioning, 'slowly, slowly,' the other devoured Mike's letters, memorising them with little difficulty – there were read so frequently!

But I had been aware of a tug of loyalties ever since our first dinner together in a London restaurant. Having only come to a firm belief that Jesus was the Son of God two years earlier, now, at twenty, my fervour as a Christian was not yet matched by maturity or sensitivity. So I launched in half way through the meal about my faith and what my conversion in Oxford in 1970 now meant to me. In a nightclub afterwards I talked loudly, about a drug centre I had been helping at as Mike winced with embarrassment. But all through the evening I had felt myself falling in love.

A puzzling thing happened as he took me back to my flat that night. He asked me if I'd go out with him again, and, though I can't get over it to this day, I said 'No'. My Christian experience so far was limited, but remembering that it simply would not work to get involved with someone who had not made a commitment to God, I can only ascribe the 'No' to the Holy Spirit's prompting. I needed time to think. When we bumped into each other on a skiing holiday in Zermatt three months later I was only too grateful for that breathing space. This was something powerful that we felt for each other, but I still wasn't sure if I was coming or going.

We had planned this summer holiday together in April, but I then wrote in June warning Mike that it might be wise if we forgot the idea. As a Christian I felt guilty, caught in a net of my own making, and I didn't want to hurt him. I was confused between my love for him, of which I had no doubt, and my love for Christ. I was unsure of my strength of character were it to become a choice between the two.

Mike replied to that on the telephone one night. 'How can you be so sure that there would be a conflict of interests? Doesn't God love me too?' To that I had no answer. But I wrote again explaining that our relationship could go no deeper whilst I was committed to Christ and he was not. It was not simply one corner of life which we did not share, rather a whole dimension which affected every aspect of my life, attitudes and priorities.

His profoundly thoughtful reply to my letter impressed me with its honesty, yet I felt I had to speak to him directly. So I found myself waiting the hour and a half it took the Italian operator to connect me to Mike's London number.

'I don't know what to say about your coming out here.' I said. 'I do,' he retorted. 'I'm coming. If you think you can stop me on the strength of a few mumblings down the telephone and some pretty muddled thinking from hundreds of miles away, you must be crazy! I want to see you and I'm going to.'

I was flattered, and threw resolve to the wind.

As soon as I arrived in Rome, I found a pensione and

went out to buy a new pair of trousers and a belt. I spent the rest of the day deciding what I wanted to see when we returned from our holiday. I was tired by eight o'clock so I set my alarm and went to bed. There was plenty of time before I was supposed to meet Mike.

But it was half past three in the morning as my yellow taxi sped along the deserted highway out to Fumicino Airport. I knew Mike's plane would have got in just before 2 am. What must he be thinking? And I'd planned everything so perfectly . . . why hadn't I woken when the alarm went off?

As I entered the airport building I saw him immediately – he stood out, so obviously British. As love stories so often say, 'my heart leapt', and I stood against a barrier for a moment to take in the fact – he was actually there. He'd fallen asleep with his wide-brimmed summer hat down over his face. Luggage and a couple of newspapers were strewn around on the adjacent seats. 'You'll have to handle this, Lord' I thought. I was mad about this man.

As the week unfolded from that airport meeting, our closeness developed into something approaching the intensity of the letters we'd exchanged all summer. We motored up the west coast, first to Porto Ercole for two days where an old man with a sun-scorched face showed us the coastline from his boat, and thence, further north to Piombino where we caught the ferry to Elba.

Some English friends in Rome had recommended a small hotel at one end of a private beach. Our room and balcony and the restaurant looked out over the sea. We were thrilled with it from the moment we saw it, and equally thrilled with each other. I was undeniably muddled about whether we ought to be on holiday together at all – let alone share a room, and I felt I was being unfair because I would not make love. Mike exercised enormous self-control, and more to keep myself on the rails than to 'convert' Mike, I played a series of David Watson cassettes on Christian commitment. We laughed at one of the guests who made no secret about observing our movements to and from the beach, with an unmistakeable glint in his eye. Little did he know!

Our relationship seemed then, and always had seemed, inevitable. Despite my narrow-minded expectation of finding a husband whose beliefs were a carbon copy of my own, a mutual awareness of a light being lit had grown until we were both convinced that the love we shared was indeed the 'real thing'. Since I had first known of Mike's existence the world had changed. It did not matter if I was not with him; the fact that he was alive, or that I had had the experience of knowing him, gave my life a new significance.

When he'd flown back to England I felt dreadfully alone. The memory of him was so powerful it seemed as though he were still with me in one sense, but I felt isolated and vulnerable, and I missed him everywhere, no matter how much I was absorbed in the beauty of my surroundings. Watching night fall over Florence from the Belvedere, I said to God: 'We have got it together from a human point of view, but can you make each of us aware if our love is a part of your plan?'

At twenty, in 1972, I was inconsistent, headstrong and a little crazy. But when, a month later, Mike was evidently moved by a challenge to faith, at a Festival of Light rally in Hyde Park, I was not only amazed, but very grateful to God for not keeping me on tenterhooks longer than was absolutely necessary! I knew Mike wanted us to get married, so when I travelled to

Scotland two days later to cook at a lodge, I went armed with writing paper and biros. Between curdling the mayonnaise, mistiming the Yorkshire pudding so it had to be eaten with golden syrup half an hour after the beef, and loading and unloading the dishwasher, I prayed and thought and walked, and wrote down the pros and cons of our getting married.

With it all laid out before me, instead of a dramatic shaft of light, I experienced a gradual peace about the pros. I walked some more, thought some more – and still felt the same. So when my contract was up I took the sleeper down to London, convinced at last that we were on the right road. As there was only a fortnight left before I was due to go up to Sheffield University, a decision of some sort was pressing. I didn't want to risk losing Mike.

The next forty-eight hours in London were filled with tiny but significant reassurances. God was in control and I was putty in his hands! Because it was a Tuesday, I was overjoyed to have an excuse to visit St Helen's in the City – the Reverend Dick Lucas's church, where I had attended lunchtime services each week when I worked near Bishopsgate. I rang Mike from a friend's house to ask if he had time to join me there.

At the close of one of Dick's characteristically telling sermons of heavenly things in our earthly language, I grabbed Mike's arm and, so as not to waste a moment of his time, we made straight for a pub I knew nearby. He found a table where it wouldn't be too noisy to talk, and ordered two chicken and chips and a salad.

A born optimist, it hadn't occurred to me that Mike might not want to marry me any more! So, once our drinks had arrived, I beamed from ear to ear, and leaned across the table to half whisper, 'Will you marry me?'

'What do you mean?' he said, straightening up in his seat.

'Exactly what I said! You told me to ask you when I was ready . . . and now I'm ready. Are you still on?' I must have begun to look worried, because he took my right hand in both of his as though it was very precious and might break.

'Of course I'm still *on* – it's just rather a shock! A moment's readjustment is needed, ma'am. I've had quite a morning one way and another in the office . . . and, well, let's just say it's not what I expected!' He kissed the top of my hand, and our food arrived. 'Well I thought I'd tell you now because there's not much time to work out what I'm going to do about Sheffield.'

'I'm going to be accused of cradle snatching!' he said and burst out laughing. Which was quite a relief. It brought some of the colour back into his cheeks.

'I thought I'd write this afternoon to Professor Atkinson in Sheffield and tell him that things have changed. Explain that the decision hasn't been made easily, but that it doesn't seem right for me to come to the university after all. What do you think?' I said.

'I don't think I think at all!' was the reply. Poor Mike was clearly flabbergasted. The plates of untouched food were pushed aside simultaneously, and he sat and stared at me, as he might have done had he known me ten years previously, and was studying how much I had changed.

'Oh, please tell me what you are thinking?' I pleaded. 'I feel pretty vulnerable. Do you love me? . . . I love you.' I had not said those words before, keeping them, so they would be special when I really meant them.

'I've loved you since the first night I took you out' he said.

'So . . . can we get married?'

'Yes, that too. You are full of surprises aren't you?' 'Actually I've often thought the same about you.' I laughed. 'You are so unpredictable, I'll never get bored!' 'I hope there's more basis to your decision than that. You're not going to change your mind?' he inquired, very serious again.

'No. All I mean by that is that I think we're both the sort of people who can cope with change, which must be important as I'm so young.'

I sipped my drink and then went on, 'I had thought we could live halfway between Sheffield and London and each commute. But the distance is too great, isn't it!'

'Yes, Twink. That's an understatement. You have a look on a map the next time you get the chance', he teased.

Reaching agreement on the incompatibility of Sheffield and wedding bells, my other chore for that afternoon was to ring round, and explore the possibilities of doing a degree in London.

By the following Tuesday my life had undergone a complete change. I was engaged to be married and, as a result of an impromptu interview at the London Bible College, I was enrolled to do a BA in Theology, beginning the next week!

Chapter 3

A double life

I had packed a lot into the last year and now I was embarking on a completely new venture. This time for study seemed the greater privilege after two years as a secretary and my spare time held all the magic and excitement I had always envisaged of an engagement. My life appeared busy with parties and fun, and my intellect, though responding with creaks and groans, was well stimulated by the lectures I attended.

In fact, the truth about *me* was a lot less attractive. I had a serious behavioural disorder of which I was deeply ashamed. I concealed it well and embarked upon a double life. Though I did not know it then, this disorder which did not emerge until I was twenty years old, had a name – bulimia nervosa. Bulimia nervosa centres on an abnormal appetite and approach to food. It may or may not be coincidental that my first recollection of displeasing grown-ups was when I found it difficult to finish what was on my plate. I can remember cramming in the last few mouthfuls of the dreaded breakfast egg and leaving the table in a great hurry to spit it down the lavatory!

Nervousness and a feeling of inadequacy in childhood

went on to contribute towards a serious stutter by the time I was eleven. For some reason, personal achievements gave me my identity. Looking back on my childhood, I can now see that I was terribly concerned with pleasing people, and measuring up. Thus if I won a race, said 'please' and 'thank you' nicely and wore a pretty party dress, I felt I had earned affection. Sifting through my early memories, I know that I received unconditional love from my family, but my mind rejected it. Perhaps my own competitive drive crowded it out, so anxious was I to achieve what I thought was expected of me.

It was while I was at boarding school in the sixties that slimming became fashionable to an unprecedented degree and, ironically, just when I was becoming clothes conscious, I was overweight for the first time in my life. With elocution classes and drama, the stutter improved and the embarrassment of getting stuck in the middle of a sentence transferred to an obsessional desire to have the 'right' shape.

While working in the City of London in 1971, I succeeded in losing ten or twelve pounds by dieting sensibly and playing tennis and squash. I had been aiming, as all dieters are apt to, for an 'ideal' weight – in my case eight and a half stone, and things might have continued as they were had I not met and found myself falling in love with Mike in the December of that year. No other man had evoked the 'must be slimmer' urge in me to such an extent. I put it down to the fact that no one else had mattered that much. And again I slipped into my childhood tendency to do something to earn affection. 'This man is getting close to me . . . and I feel inadequate. What have I to offer him? Am I worth anything as a person?' My mind worked it all out and came up with a solution: get thin, because thin is lovable. Feel fat and . . . ugh!

I was in the middle of an identity crisis. Unable to accept myself other than in those moments of supreme effort when I became something which I was not, I felt permanently exhausted by acting out various roles, and I loathed myself.

The prospect of my first date with Mike, dinner on a Friday evening, had injected a 'life and death' urgency into my dieting. I ate very little all week. At six o'clock after work on 'the' day I was starved so I began nibbling apples and cheese and, in so doing, realised that I had no confidence about the coming evening. Blaming myself, I went on to eat some bread and butter and chocolate biscuits. All foods which I usually denied myself. They were categorised as 'no-no's', and I associated them with comfort and feeling full, sensations I tried to avoid.

That was *it*! Now my diet was ruined, and I would look and feel fat to add insult to injury – I only felt good when my stomach was empty. I calculated that there was enough time for me to eat as much as I wanted and afterwards maybe try to make myself sick. I knew people did that sometimes, and it was worth attempting. I just had to be thin tonight . . . no matter what. So there began the ultimate contradiction: I wanted to be thin, but I ate and ate.

Even now I can still see the blurred picture I had of the lavatory bowl on that first occasion, and feel the involuntary reaction to my attempts to retch. I felt grotesque and heavy, and was terrified that one of my flatmates might arrive back and discover me.

I was emotionally exhausted and very relieved when, finally, I vomited. Emptying my body of the calories I had consumed. I felt that I had at last found the back-stop to slimming which would work for me. Long term I had rarely won the diet war, but tonight, triggered off by the need for an instant remedy, I thought I had found a way out of the consequences of over-eating. What a release! It was to be *my secret.*

In reality, far from being an answer, from the outset it was squalid and awful. It worked passably in Italy, where I lost another stone. I convinced myself that I had this bizarre habit under control and the devious ways in which I managed to be on my own had not, as yet, struck me as dishonest.

Then, on my return to England, everything went completely sour. In London it seemed as though people could see right through me. Everywhere I went people commented on my shape.

'My golly! Is it really Lissa? You look completely different.'

'How much weight have you lost?'

'How did you do it?'

The world's comments about my slimmer figure evoked well-rehearsed, nonchalant replies. I could hear my own voice telling blatant untruths and I began to feel so body conscious that even 'You look great' seemed threatening.

Social events, even informal suppers, proved such a strain that soon my behaviour became viciously uncontrollable. I was dieting for as long as I could, binge-vomiting and then returning to the diet, and I found I could no longer use the procedure like that . . . it was using me. No longer was it a tension release valve which I could put off for a time by taking exercise or finding a diversion. I now depended on the 'high' before the vomit and I was spending increasingly large sums of money on food to achieve it. I gave in to it as soon as the idea presented itself and allocated whole mornings for the sordid business of buying, eating and vomiting enormous quantities of those foods which I had mentally categorised as being greedy treats. Within a comparatively short time I had put on weight and began then to blame myself for being a fraud, and an inefficient one: the scheming and expense which went towards providing time and food for such sessions was achieving nothing. I was not losing weight. The emotions I could not express in my daily living were all vented during the agonised hours of these eat-then-vomit sessions. But it was all turned inwards at me. I felt an unquenchable anger against the world, and an impotence to express it in any other way than this furtive abuse of my system.

Subconsciously, I knew all this within weeks of getting back to London. Things went from bad to worse and I had one session, a few days before my twenty-first birthday which was horrific. Indescribable. Moreover, such experiences became commonplace in my life, and although they frightened me at the time, I am now even more appalled when I remember what was involved. I was like a madman bent on self-destruction. Eating the first few mouthfuls with little enjoyment, and the rest with none. I would talk menacingly at myself – cynically jibing that I had one thing only in common with Saint Paul . . . I was always doing exactly what I didn't want to do. When these warped encounters with my feelings were over, and vomiting had made my tensions disappear, for a time at least, I felt like a piece of chewed string. My stomach was sore and I had an extraordinary sensation of pumping, even shaking, which seemed to come from my chest. Yet afterwards I never once took the pressure off by giving myself a chance to sit down and rest. I would feverishly repair the blotchy face and re-apply the mask of self-sufficiency. Whatever was visible to my friends, only God knew the turmoil inside me. I was struggling to reconcile my dual personality: the secret me, and the public me, and I was unsure if either was genuine.

This was where I had got to during my first term at Bible College, except that the bad sessions became increasingly frequent. The pressures of my close relationship with Mike and trying to settle on some method of study made the charade harder to sustain. I was deeply unhappy and confused.

Paradoxically, instead of managing to keep track of my eating habits, I had instead entirely lost control of my appetite and was now consuming larger and larger quantities before being sick. What was more I had come to see it as my right, almost, to allow myself an opportunity to vomit at the slightest feeling of hurt or disappointment, but I so disgusted myself that I could not face telling anyone.

By the end of that first term, last year's tension valve had become a prison. My life was pervaded by despair. I was trapped in a vicious circle, at the centre of which was *the* priority: *at all costs be thin.*

Slamming the car door shut on most of the noise of enthusiastic students wishing each other, and me, a Happy Christmas, I pulled out into the traffic winding its way towards the A40 into Central London, feeling desperate. It was pouring and my own tears mingled with the torrential rain on the windscreen. Car headlights blurred and I completed the journey with difficulty.

Sleep eluded me for hours that night. I was staring at

myself, seeing the insidious penetration of my illness into every aspect of my lifestyle. I could no longer kid myself. I was suffering from a life-threatening condition. I had no energy. I was highly nervous, moody, and frequently felt dizzy, blacking out for seconds at a time. It seemed as though my heart had manufactured a new and frightening pulse, it thumped through my chest and stomach, and I trembled and began noticing my hand shaking when I picked up a pen to write or reached out for a glass at a party. Yet still I pushed myself to the utmost limits – swimming, walking, entertaining, pretending to everyone, even to Mike . . . and I frankly did not know where it would end, or even if it was stoppable.

As I lay there I wondered how God could fit into this muddled jigsaw which my life had become. I felt the more a traitor to my own body because of my Christian experience, and considered that it might be easier if I was an atheist. There would still be pressure, but different pressure and less of it. Why had God not stepped in to help? I knew in my heart of hearts that He cared . . . so why was He not getting through to me? I'd often said to Him, 'Well, here we go again, Lord . . .' In some sense I longed to talk to someone but the horror of anyone finding out what I was really like prevented me.

Then the words 'Fear not' came into my mind . . . to be affirmed several minutes later. As I was beginning to drift off to sleep, thinking that I had probably imagined the comfort they gave, they became more distinct . . . and seemed to be addressing my whole being. I must have retained the thought all night, because on waking I honestly felt, for the first time, that I must share my anguish and depression with someone. It was as if after making a conscious decision to find the right person a great weight had been lifted from me . . . 'Fear not' was all the encouragement I needed to step out of my isolation.

I knew almost immediately to whom I would turn. She was someone of whom I was already fond, a dependable Christian, a few years older than myself, whose deep understanding of life's problems had made her instrumental in helping many people. She became a close friend, and though I nearly cancelled that first appointment, I eventually found myself in her Kensington drawing room on a sunny afternoon in February 1973. Sitting on the edge of my seat, drinking coffee, I hoped that she would not reject me after my confession.

It was difficult to know where to start. By this time, Mike and I had planned our wedding, so I told her I couldn't imagine being able to live at close quarters with him because I had an eating problem which hinged on a compulsion like that of alcoholism. Although I didn't tell her, I was terrified of what marriage might reveal about me.

'I am sure lots of alcoholics go through far worse than me, but I'm so depressed; I feel jealous of them because they can stop drinking, and never *have* to take alcohol again whereas I am faced with eating every day for the rest of my life.'

I was talking very fast, everything gushing out in no logical order. She sat there opposite me, twiddling the rings on one finger, just listening.

'You see,' I went on, 'I can't stop eating sometimes. And by that I don't mean what other people mean. I started off by my making myself sick after an eating binge. Now I can't stop, it has become a prop, and it's ruining my life. I feel lost, and I can't go on. It affects my concentration, at the bank I'm heavily overdrawn, and I swing unpredictable from one mood to the next.

I've lost all my enthusiasm for life. Mike is marrying . . . well, a nothing.'

There was a heavy silence, which she interrupted with emphasis. 'Can I tell you for sure that you are not alone. There is a hope which is certain. God longs to heal you and to help you find your real self. Thank you for trusting me so far. There is someone I may want to refer to if we are going to meet every week, and anything I discussed with him would be in the strictest confidence.' She looked at me for my response, so I nodded, and without pausing she went on, 'We will work at this thing together, but about which particular aspect of it do you feel the most guilty? The money, the wasted time or what?'

'Everything,' I whispered, in tears.

We drank more coffee and I told her about the verse a friend had written in the front of my Bible. It said that God has given us a spirit of power and love and self-control,* and I had stopped reading my Bible because it taunted me. Nothing could be farther removed from my life of lies. I explained, 'I seem to be caught up in a twenty-four hour a day preoccupation with what I eat, and how to lie my way out of eating what I don't want to eat. I tell lies to anyone, to everyone . . . and it's like a malignant cancer, which has already spread to other areas of my life.'

She was very understanding but it was not so much what she said, it was her acceptance. She loved me throughout, proving unshockable. She listened as though I was the only person in the world who mattered to her, and in her I met that unconditional love I was eventually to learn that God has for me.

*2 Tim. 1:7 For the Spirit that God has given us does not make us timid; instead, his Spirit fills us with power, love and self-control.

Mike and I were married two months later in April 1973. Looking back to our first five years together, the worst years for me as an individual, and for our marriage as a result, I am frankly amazed by them. I went so low for so long that it was at times unbearable, and for that reason I suspect I might not have recovered had it not been for this friend and one other, an equally busy counsellor. They both frequently squeezed me in to hectic schedules, often at short notice. Their support was rock-like, steady and yet creative, so that I never left either of them without something to think on – even at the bottom of the pit they made me acknowledge each tiny encouragement.

It began to filter through to me: No matter what you think of yourself, God has not rejected you.

Chapter 4

'For worse'

Naturally inclined to push myself too hard, bulimia added an intolerable burden to my over-busy life, and the pressure escalated in the May of 1973, when, after seven weeks of marriage, I had to sit my first year's exams.

Mike came upstairs one evening to find me sitting in bed, crying my heart out. 'I have barely read the text in English, let alone the Greek' I sobbed. 'How can I possibly go into a three hour exam tomorrow?' His behaviour somewhat approaching that of a benevolent uncle, Mike sat me on his lap and taught me an exam psychology which got me through those first year papers. That minor drama was apparent to us both. But there were many more problems brewing beneath the surface, some of which were a direct result of bulimia nervosa, and others were exacerbated by my condition.

We had decided, at the beginning of my course, to try to keep home life as normal as possible, but I got very, very tired. I got up most mornings before seven because lectures were sixteen miles away. Permanently exhausted from the illness, let alone studying and running the house, when we entertained or went out for dinner I was shattered. Yet I went because Mike needed to relax away from the office and I needed a break from studying. Unfortunately with such low self-esteem I never differentiated between what we should do and what I frankly should have declined.

I seemed to fall between every stool. I did not find the academic work easy and I was trying, mainly through culinary disasters, to learn to cook! My lack of method at housework was matched only by lack of enthusiasm. When Mike complained that his asthma was not responding well to the build-up of dust mites, he'd push the vacuum-cleaner around himself rather than face the unequal struggle of trying to persuade me. Ironing piled up in mounds, and more often than not ended up under the spare room bed, because I'd make a frantic effort to tidy up if we had friends coming round. Mike went frequently to Marks and Spencer to stock his drawers in a desperate attempt to forestall the daily rows about there being no clean shirts, pants or socks!

The weekends, when Mike wanted to unwind from the office, and I had overdue essays to write, became, inevitably, times of bitter exchanges. Resentments which had built up during the week found their outlet in petty wranglings, but I did not argue rationally . . . I just bickered and when he 'made up' and was loving, I was often still harbouring grudges and rejected him.

One Sunday during my three year degree course was typical of our 'days of rest'.

'It's two o'clock, are we eating lunch today?' Mike peered into the drawing room, where I was surrounded by quantities of untidy notes, text books, empty mugs of coffee and discarded first paragraphs. 'Oh golly, is that really the time!' I exclaimed, feigning surprise. 'I won't be long.'

I got to my feet and hurried to the kitchen where I fried two chicken legs, and made up some Smash. There was salad left over from the night before which I plonked in the middle of the kitchen table. Then, anxious to appear less disorganised than I was, I called out, 'Are you ready – lunch is served!'

'This is supposed to be my home too, you know,' Mike began, pulling out his chair to sit down. 'I can't get into the bedroom for all the clutter, blankets and books on top of the bed, and the mess in the drawing room is ridiculous'.

'I know, I am sorry,' I said, and I was. 'But anyway, here's some food' – hoping like mad that he'd drop the subject. But he didn't.

'If you'd get on with it when you decided to work then you'd be finished at a sensible time and we could have some kind of life together. As it is you wander around half the morning making cups of coffee instead of getting down to it . . . it's all very well . . .' He paused to look at my plate. 'Aren't you eating?'

'No, I'm not hungry, I had a huge breakfast!' I lied.

'I can't believe you really need all those books out at once. You're completely chaotic. And what on earth is this? You haven't cooked this chicken at all . . . look at it. I can't eat that, it's red, not even warm in the middle.' He prodded it with his knife and fork.

He got up in disgust and slammed the front door as he left the house. I was desolate. I did not appreciate then, just how miserable I had made Mike. Unknown to each other at the time, we were each praying in desperation, 'Please may this be "for worse" and can "for better" come soon.'

Blindly I set my sights on being 'a little bit thinner'. I told myself that everything would be different if I weighed less. Mike would adore me, and I would be tremendously fit and caring. So I even sent off for some slimming pills, and wasted away further, getting tireder, though less tense, because I had so little energy left. It was an uphill struggle, concealing bulimia nervosa day in and day out, deceiving Mike for two years.

And he went on loving me. Insecure at times himself, he nonetheless remained faithful and kind, and we were still very much attracted to each other. So when I was settled in a job in London, a year after graduation we decided to start a family. Mike could not possibly have known at that stage how ill I was. Both make-up and clothes were studied and chosen to create exactly the effect I wanted, but my weight had dropped below eight stone and I could not remember when I had last had a period.

The weeks and then months went by, until eventually after talking to Mike about it, I looked up the name of the only gynaecologist I had recently heard of and made an appointment.

In the centre of his room in Harley Street stood a solid oak desk, covered with green leather. It exactly suited the big man whose arms weighed upon it, and I liked him as soon as I saw him. He resembled an overgrown teddy bear . . . the sort of man some women mistakenly try to reform!

He motioned me to a chair, and smiled as he began inquiring about my medical and specifically gynaecological history. All his movements, even the way he shifted his weight to get more comfortable in the chair, were slow. He was large and forthright and I could immediately tell that this man was not going to buoy me up with any kind of false hope.

The complete antithesis of his confident untidiness, I

sat there immaculately turned out but terribly nervous. I was willing to do anything that might give me the chance of having a child. Anything, that was, except put on weight.

Despite having no tangible encouragement, I left feeling positive and spent my homeward journey going through the main points which had arisen. He had warned me off taking my temperature – apparently it would be counter-productive in my case, merely worsening the tension and until I was ovulating there was no point in a temperature chart. He explained that the reason for amenorrhoea* had to be established as the first priority. I was the sort of person who ought never to have taken the contraceptive pill, but no matter. I had not taken it during the last three years so there were drugs that he would expect to work quite quickly. A laparoscopy (insertion of a lens with a light through a small incision below my navel) would tell him all he needed to know about my ovaries and tubes.

As I drove I remembered him explaining, 'I don't believe in keeping couples holding on, one pill one month and another six months later. The strain takes its toll on the relationship. With a rest on alternate months, you will have everything in the book over a period of about eighteen months . . . and if we are not successful, you and your husband will be forced to face up to the likelihood that you never will have a baby.'

His saying those unmentionable words had the same effect as a surgeon's lancet would on an infected wound. The panic, just like the poison, began to drain away. I was left with a problem, but it was of more acceptable proportions. The future was to be faced straight on, one step at a time. He would dictate the

* failure of menstruation.

pace, so I could be more objective about the whole thing.

Although I was depressed the difference that being a Christian made during this period was that I came to situations trusting that God would sustain me through those little 'throw-aways' that another, less introspective person might have failed to notice. Even the gynaecologist's '. . . and if we are not successful' was a comfort. It was almost God saying *we*–'I am in this with you, you are not alone.' I had taken God at His word. I couldn't see how He would achieve it, but I believed I was getting better so I held on to that even when the bulimia got worse.

I had the laparoscopy, which left me sore for a couple of days, but relieved to hear that my insides looked healthy. Next on the agenda was to check out the quantity and quality of what Mike was 'firing'.

Semen samples have to be tested quickly so Mike arranged to see the urologist, and came to the appropriate building on the appointed morning. 'Where is your sample Mr Shortt?' the receptionist asked. 'I was told I could do it here' Mike replied. 'But you can't!' she stammered 'I m-mean we only have one lavatory'.

Apparently Mike then said 'It's all right, I am not going to be in there all morning'. With which he disappeared towards the door marked toilet, re-emerging only minutes later to the astonishment of the receptionist! To our great relief, the results of that test were excellent.

During the first month of treatment I took the pills, a low dose of chlomiphene, and we abstained from sex from the seventh to the twelfth day of the month. As I marked my diary in advance, we made love on the twelfth, fourteenth and sixteenth days. It seemed to present no awesome problem! I made more of a feature of supper and we had a couple of glasses of wine . . . and got on with it.

However, making love to order was not always possible. Two months later, staying with friends in Yorkshire, we were forced, by a combination of paper-thin walls, dog hairs (which aggravated Mike's asthma), and a bitterly cold room, to abandon the project! 'Let's just cuddle – we can make babies tomorrow', Mike said. 'Fine' I agreed, and we fell asleep in each other's arms.

I am not sure whether it was my embarrassment at having my legs up in stirrups for the tests which were done two weeks later, or whether it was just the disappointment when I didn't conceive, but for whatever reason the tension increased again after that walking holiday in Yorkshire. I punished myself by more rigorous dieting, resulting in the worst spell of overeating and vomiting yet. I was back in the pit of self-punishment. I had not got out of it but, I had for a while been hopeful. Now I again saw my body as hideous, incurable and infertile . . . an empty shell. I wanted a baby and normality – normality and a baby. In my mind the two were linked. For a time I felt that wherever I went, to whichever counsellor, now even to the gynaecologist, I let people down. I could not have twenty-four hour surveillance, yet that was what I needed.

I was keeping a notebook of insights and promises which might one day contribute towards my recovery, but there was a long period, more than six months, when I felt that I had let God down so dramatically, I wondered how much longer I could go on believing in Him. I had talked glibly to friends about His perfect timing, but having long since given up hope of an overnight cure, I thought perhaps this was one situation God couldn't handle.

Not long after, the consultant referred me to Guy's as a National Health outpatient. I arrived at the clinic feeling good – having managed not to eat at all for two days. Here I answered yet more intimate questions about my menstrual history and present sex life . . . which was conspicuous by its absence. I was told that my treatment would be intensified.

Then the following week I was introduced to the biochemist who was ultimately to play the most important role in keeping me sane. I never had to tell her what I was feeling; she read it in my face and, whilst understanding, she never alluded to it. For a fortnight before the HCG jabs* (part of the fertility treatment), and during the span of six days when I had the three injections, spaced out, I had to collect twenty-four hour urine specimens. I delivered these to her personally, which gave me a link with the person who was testing for my hormone levels, and was anticipating my ovulating with as much enthusiasm as I. She was in every sense a friend. Full of hope and encouragement.

I took the huge bottles and a funnel everywhere with me while I was doing these 'collections'. Out to dinner, to friends' houses and restaurants, Wimbledon Lawn Tennis Championships, Covent Garden, Chelsea Football Ground, shopping . . . The time I found hardest to remember was in the middle of the night, if we had been late to bed!

Although it was a bore, the funnel and large plastic bottles made Mike and me see the funny side of my predicament! Through everything, what we shared and

*human chorionic gonadotrophin.

what we could not, arguments, differences of opinion, having few interests in common, Mike and I were still friends. Experience had shown me so far that our marriage needed encouraging rather like one would egg on a cyclist . . . you miss out on the views if your guts and strength give out before the top of the hill.

There was no greater test for our friendship than the problem we came up against in January 1977, as a result of 'scheduled intercourse' becoming impossible. For many months I had been writing in my diary, weeks in advance, when we could not have sex, and the three days when we must have sex. One particular night highlighted for us exactly how far removed the sex act had become from what God had intended. There was no spontaneity or enjoyment. It left us depressed and despairing. We lay there staring at the ceiling in silence, the atmosphere loaded with resentment, rejection, hate even.

When I arrived at Guy's the next morning with my two urine bottles and stepped out of the lift I virtually bumped into the biochemist. 'Will you ring me tonight?' she said. 'You'll be needing another injection I expect, but I shan't know for sure until I've checked these. There's a good chance, from your graph so far, that you ovulated yesterday.' I knew I had to tell her, but I felt dreadfully embarrassed, as I blurted out, 'We couldn't do it last night. We tried, but we didn't have sex . . . we couldn't. Sex to order is impossible. It's horrid and degrading. It just makes us feel resentful. I feel awful, especially when I think of all that you and the doctors have done for us.' I perched on a stool and cried.

'Okay', she said, without showing any disappointment. 'If you come to the casualty entrance at seven thirty tonight I'll arrange for a doctor to meet you, and you can have AIH. That is AI Husband. Don't make yourself feel worse. You're doing fine.'

Arriving at the hospital on time, everything seemed all right until we caught sight of the doctor. Poor man, he was unsure of himself and frankly more embarrassed than we were.

'Where is the sample?' he addressed Mike without looking at him.

'I've come straight from work.'

'You can go in there,' he said, indicating the Gents' lavatory. Mike gaped at me but I was reacting slowly to all this, completely nonplussed by the whole business.

With hardly enough room to turn around, staring into a lavatory that had not flushed for some time, he re-emerged ten minutes later and said forcefully, 'This is impossible. It's inhuman to expect us to go along with this. Come on Lissa, we're going home.' It was a statement of fact.

Not that month, but the one after, I conceived. It was a month when I took no pills and was given no injections, a rest for my ovaries. So, without the pressure of pre-planned sex, we found ourselves wanting to make love again. On one of those nights life began for our first child – it was to end in stillbirth.

About four and a half years elapsed from the worsening of my illness in the autumn of 1972 to the day I walked into our Fulham semi after giving death to our baby. It had been a shock, one minute carrying the baby, the next in labour and now . . . with nothing. I wished I had just a tiny rattle, a shawl – there was nothing to have a good howl over. We had not bought a thing, almost as though we had anticipated this.

I threw my bag on the side and crossed the kitchen to the glazed door. The garden, begun with love, was now well established and I resented its lushness, that it should have the audacity to flourish in the face of our tragedy. It lacked empathy for my unhappy womb.

I took a limp lettuce out of the fridge and opened a tin of tuna fish. There were one and a half tomatoes. 'Pathetic,' I said aloud. But it would have to be lunch.

We ate in the garden, unenthusiastically. Talking about the weather being overcast to match our mood, and other trivia. We weren't able to help each other. Didn't really even feel the inclination. For the time being we were locked into out personal sorrow, and it was different for each of us.

The full experience of sadness impinged more on Mike than on me; a more spontaneous person, his loss was written on his face, and obvious in his tired voice. He was devastated. Yet for me a kind of numbness had set in, I found myself cut off, in a distant, contemplative world. I was unable to grieve in any deep sense.

When Mike went back to work after a few days, I was alone in the house from eight in the morning until six at night. Emotionally volatile, I swung between feeling thrilled that I had been pregnant, that my womb had nurtured life, knowing that I had transmitted a powerful love to that child . . . to then confronting my illness. I found it even harder to cope with it in the face of this tragic disappointment. Feeling a failure it became a habit to be hard on myself, at times, cruel – 'Don't pretend. Whatever anyone else might say, you know the truth! People who treat their bodies the way you do can't expect to have healthy babies.' Neighbours and friends were kind and invited me to lunch. Usually I went, but always, whatever the circumstances, alone or in company, I got more lonely and I felt I was back at square one, with no child. The only difference being that I now knew I could conceive, although I knew it would mean embarking on more hormone treatment, because I had not menstruated for three and a half years.

Happily however, the treatment worked a second time and after more pills and injections in 1978 I found myself pregnant again.

Chapter 5

Add Lucinda . . . make a family?

The care with which we had planned how far I should or should not travel in my first pregnancy had proved pointless. So this time I went everywhere and did everything! In 1978 when I was fourteen weeks pregnant we flew to Los Angeles to spend a month in the States. We went to Disneyland, flew to Las Vegas for two days and by mid-June had arrived at Yosemite National Park.

Yosemite in June is indescribable. A glory of nature, with fast melting ice adding to the full flow of the cascading falls. We took some stunning photographs with no effort, and fell in love with the place.

The height of the mountains and the depth of the lower land, the grassy meadows, reminded me of the contrasts in our experiences so far. What we lacked was roots like the giant sequoia trees we saw, solid and dependable. Or perhaps our roots were there in a battered but enduring friendship . . . just in need of nourishment. That scenery challenged us. No matter what had gone before, here and now was vital and provided us with the perfect background for enjoying the present.

The mass of the mountains humbled us and prompted us to rethink certain perspectives in life. We walked and talked, taking in the sheer pleasures of being alive and rediscovering our companionship.

Some months previously I had summoned enough courage to tell Mike about my illness and it was not as harrowing as I had feared. He was understanding and helpful despite being shocked, and I had made some steps towards relearning the sensations of hunger and satisfaction. After leaving Yosemite, I chalked up two firsts. One was in Sacramento City, where I indulged in a lot of chocolate chip cookies and chocolate shakes . . . without being sick afterwards! The second experience was when I ate and enjoyed a second helping of marinated lamb in peanut sauce in a very exclusive restaurant in San Francisco! How ridiculous to put so much emphasis on two such trivial events. But as I had been so ill, every milestone passed was a powerful indication of God's healing in me. I praised Him for it and shared the victories with Mike.

'Can you believe it?' I tugged on Mike's arm as we crossed the road outside a lamb and beef grill in Reno.

'Believe what?' he asked.

'I had a baked potato tonight. Did you notice?'

'I can't say I did.'

'Well it was yum and I had butter and sour cream on it . . . and I feel delicously full but I'm not running away from the feeling. I don't even want to be sick. I really am getting better. Maybe I'm getting the help from "somewhere else" to do the baby good.'

So a potato had marked another historical breakthrough! I was not programmed to expect such a mundanity to be important evidence of a healing process, but I recorded it in the memory bank, and opened my heart a little wider. 'Please God, do it your way . . . whatever that is, and I will try to trust you.'

Five months passed before I was again in labour. The date was 7 November 1978. I had been in the delivery room in Guy's since midnight, when I had been rushed to hospital in an ambulance after strong contractions during a performance of *Evita!*

In between pushing till I could almost see the purple blood vessels on my own face, I noticed Mike standing behind my left shoulder, he looked miserable. Sister glanced at him, then away again, her silence intentional. There were now several people in the room. Three more had bustled in with an incubator.

'Fine,' I thought, and then, 'Not so fine! What on earth is that?'

Information was immediately forthcoming:

'These are Neville Barnes forceps,' the doctor explained. 'I'm glad I never saw *them* before,' I thought. 'There are some advantages to ignorance and premature labour!'

I gave one last push and then the lovely Sister, who had been through it all with us last time, addressed Mike first, 'You have a daughter, Mr Shortt.' Inopportunely, in this moment of triumph – he was blowing his nose like a foghorn!

They checked her over briefly then handed her to me. I felt very proud, but equally clumsy!

'Hello Lucinda,' I managed. For a moment longer I held her awkwardly and self-consciously. Mike leaned against the bed to look closely at her too, and we were rendered speechless! Longing to convey love to her, yet embarrassed by a combination of awe and inexperience.

She was taken down to Special Care, because of her lungs were not fully mature at thirty-five weeks, and she was having some difficulty breathing. I was wheeled to the ward, where I broke down from a sense of relief and the sight of so many mothers with their babies beside them.

'I'm sorry,' I said turning to the orderly and staff nurse, 'but my last baby died . . .' I paused, looking round at the five little bundles in their cots, 'and my baby is downstairs.' I did not need to say any more. Thankfully, there was an amenity room I could go straight into, where I fell into a deep dreamless sleep.

The birth had been scary for me. I had known nothing about breathing, and no one had ever described to me what labour pains were like. The experience had been negative for Mike too. Pacing up and down the same corridor where he had mourned our first baby, his face showed he was reliving that horror.

After her safe delivery, though medically Lucinda was in no danger, the first glimpse I had of her, in her incubator, brought a lump to my throat. Instead of joy and maternal instinct, I felt appalled. Covered in lanugo (hair) her whole body struggled in concert with her lungs as they worked double-time to fill with enough air. 'What have I done,' I thought, 'giving birth to this poor little thing, who is already suffering after only a few hours of life? Maybe we should not have persevered, and been content with no children.'

'I'll get your baby out for you, Mrs Shortt,' the nurse said briskly. I stammered, 'Oh, n-no, d-don't!' She started to dress Lucinda who began crying, and her breathing became more rapid. 'You're upsetting her,' I said. At that very moment Sister came in. 'Now, Mrs

Shortt, all babies need their mothers.' I stood rigid, bemused by the tube and the probe to monitor her temperature. And I found myself asking: 'Is this what I have been waiting for?' I bathed her in tears, not of love, but of apprehension.

After that initial outburst I found I was easily reassured by the paediatrician and other hospital staff. She came out of her incubator after six days and we were home when she was two weeks old. Her contentment was a joy, but Mike's concern continued beyond that first week, and it became apparent early on that we were not in agreement on the subject of Lucinda's health and well-being. Though we tried, our past experience of illness jarred. Each of us brought to the care and discussion of Lucinda's health our separate and entirely polarised attitudes. If the devil needed any area at which to pummel away and break down our lines of communication, he did not need to look very far. Here was a ready-made breach. Particularly as Lucinda suffered cold after cold, most of which went to her chest that first winter. Mike had spent three months in hospital with a lung abscess when he was six and that combined with the experience of severe asthma attacks to produce a pessimistic, over-cautious approach to illness. My mother's caring calm, and my comparatively healthy childhood made me conversely casual. We were, subconsciously, if not openly, at war!

Because I was depressed I was short on judgement. I knew it but would not admit as much to Mike. His panics about Lucinda's flu and chesty coughs irritated me, and I obstinately assured him, 'She's okay, stop flapping.' There *were* times when Mike was over-anxious, but I can remember making several thoughtless mistakes which made him even more concerned about her well-being.

We were now in possession of a gorgeous little girl and should have been rejoicing. But the bulimia and its resultant deception, had separated me from my friends. So I had no one to turn to when Mike and I found we could not adjust to the problems of parenthood.

A country lover at heart, I have always needed to be out of doors for some part of the day, and it did not help my depression having to keep Lucinda indoors. It was a bitterly cold winter, with heavy falls of snow in London, and when it was not snowing or blowing sheets of rain, it was foggy and the fog crept across the Bishop's Park from the Thames to warn me not to take her out. Mike left home at eight in the morning, so Lucinda and I had a long day together, alone. I was engulfed in a paralysing depression which left me tired even if I had slept for eight hours. I mooched around between Lucinda's feeds, feeling guilty that I was unappreciative of her, and desperately disappointed that one big fantasy had been blown . . . nothing had changed. Despite having a child I was still throwing up with alarming regularity.

I read and re-read parts of Solzhenitsyn's *The Gulag Archipelago*, and realised that I knew the experience of 'solitary' and just how effective it was in wearing one down. When I thought of my friends they seemed distant – they coped, I did not. It was that simple. I became more isolated. Oh, I did see some of them . . . two quite regularly, but I lied about what I was really feeling like. I could not do other than that – I could no longer distinguish even between truth and exaggeration.

Having explained the background, I ought to say that Lucinda was a 'model' baby. She sucked well, burped immediately afterwards and went back to sleep without any fuss. Each time she woke for a feed she was alert and pleased to see me, and her response to and imitation of my facial expressions were a delight. She always spent the morning in her pram after she was about five months old.

An improvement in the weather that spring, 1979, coincided with the end of her last chest infection that winter, and the warmer weather lifted my spirits. I needed a break. One day I looked at my watch at 1.30 pm and decided it was time to go and get her up. 'Lucinda, . . . it's lunchtime, darling. Come on, Lucinda Bear, you've been looking at that tree for two hours!' I conjured a warmth and a teasing into my voice as I stepped out through the French windows onto the lawn. The day was mild, April sunshine falling into our leafy garden. I coaxed Lucinda again, 'Come on – wakey, wakey!' But I could see she was awake.

As I walked round the pram and stood in front of the apple tree she was studying, she caught sight of me and her grin, as ever, melted my heart and soothed away the exhaustion of the morning's housework. A pixie with a comb of 'punky' black hair, that would *not* lie down, she had such an aminated and alert little expression, her enthusiasm and innocence were disarming.

I released the safety harness and swept her out of the pram. We danced round, my baby suspended in my outstretched arms. Then we hugged, squeezing our bodies to tightly together, I felt we were one. 'I love you, I love you, my little bear,' I whispered behind her ear as we walked into the kitchen. She chuckled, and her body wriggled with the tickling of my whisper.

Confidence of manner and my cheerful voice belied deeper feelings as I warmed Lucinda's lunch. I was concerned about her failure to respond when I called her. This was not the first time, but I had previously put it down to our living in the flight path for Heathrow.

Today, I realised, there had been no planes. The winter having dragged Mike and me through a hell of argument and misunderstanding, I thought I'd keep this to myself for a while . . . it was far too controversial.

As I pondered, I remembered sensing something odd about Lucinda's response to noise while she was in her incubator. At the time I had not only noticed but commented on the effect the flip-top bin had each time it banged shut. Lucinda always jumped, clearly so startled she would move down in her glass 'box'. Yet none of the other three babies moved or showed any sign of having heard it. It was as though that sound somehow disturbed what was, for Lucinda, an otherwise peaceful world.

I did not want to pursue such an uncomfortable avenue of thinking that afternoon. So I scraped the mucky food off her chin, drained my mug of coffee and sat her in a bouncer, so that I could listen to *Woman's Hour* while I washed up. I was juggling with two thoughts: that Lucinda was an adorable little girl, unusually fascinated by the world around her; and that she seemed not to hear as I did.

It was the following Saturday afternoon, over a cup of tea, that Mike remarked, 'Has it ever struck you that for such a young baby Lucinda seems very bright?'

'A genuine throw-back to real brains you mean?' I joked.

'I don't know about that, but I'm serious – it's her face, she's far more alert than any other baby I've known.'

'That's just it!' I said. 'We haven't known many babies well. At least not at this age. I can't think of a comparison.'

'You don't think she's odd? Tell me, honestly?'

If I had not spent a vast chunk of the day in a panic

about the forthcoming evening, I should have welcomed a chance to talk this thing through. Lucinda was extraordinarily visually aware, searching her surroundings and our faces every two minutes or so. But jumpy and miserable as I was that day, I failed to see his concern for what it was. Whenever we discussed health my hackles went up, as I now over-reacted to his question.

'Of course I don't think she's odd! Goodness me, we've been longing – literally living – to have a child. Now we've got one and she's a bit special and you are talking about her being odd. I'm taking her up for a bath. I must get on because we have got all those people coming for supper . . . remember? Someone has got to do the cooking.'

As I walked heavily up the stairs I actually heard him say, 'Not odd, but different.' There was not a trace of malice in his voice, which made me the more guilty about the barb in my own remark.

Lucinda gurgled and splashed in the bath, but my mind was elsewhere. Why was it always my fault, why did I stop conversations dead in their tracks? I was so discontented, so unhappy . . . and hypercritical of Mike, myself and other people. Again, I had ruined a chance to talk, as I had ruined countless others, because of my resentment. I felt Mike was unable to understand my fatigue . . . he had never tried to look after a child, a home, entertain and act out a flawless masquerade.

Just as I was unable then to face events or emotions which needed thinking through, I later opted out of making an objective assessment of Lucinda's failure to form sounds and I blotted out the significance of the eight month and ten month hearing tests, which were unsuccessful.

'This sort of child who is very visually aware is always

difficult to test,' had been the verdict. So I had been prepared to leave it at that. I couldn't face more. I was told to expect a card from the hospital giving me the date and time of a more extensive investigation of her hearing, sometime in the new year. But the appointment never came. When Mike discovered that I'd done nothing about following it up, he insisted that I rang immediately to arrange another date.

When Lucinda was tested as thoroughly as was possible for her seventeen months, she seemed very deaf indeed, but because she had a heavy cold, the audiologist explained that she was likely to have a lot of 'glue' in her middle ear. I remember leaving the hospital hoping that the problem was all catarrh, but we were warned from the outset that such a low level of hearing might be attributable to nerve deafness. The ENT consultant would not favour operating at her age, but she could have two hearing aids which she needed for speech development.

The following day we went to the coast. That holiday was largely spent watching Lucinda. Her responses and her cleverly evolved ways of compensating for the hearing loss. So many of her responses were ambiguous – she was keen, even at eighteen months, not to be left out of anything – she would play us along until it became impossible for her to pretend any further that she had not heard what had originally been said. We realised how loudly we spoke too, in fact, shouted would be more appropriate, and we were amazed that we could have failed to appreciate the extent of her problem. We sat on the beach as Lucinda learned to wield a spade, always hoping that the worst of the loss came from the 'glue'.

Our attention was temporarily diverted. Upon our

return to London, Lucinda's ear moulds were ready and at a year and a half her world was amplified. She was *thrilled* and had none of the horror of the aids which I first felt. The second day she wore them she woke up from her morning rest and gesticulated wildly for me to put them in again . . . *she* helped *me* over that psychological hurdle.

It was another eighteen months before we went to hospital to have her adenoids taken out, the 'glue' drained and grommets put into each ear. For fun, Lucinda and I had a bath together the morning after her operation. I tried talking to her without raising my voice . . . but she could not hear me. Her hearing was still very down on what we had hoped. She was partially deaf: her considerable hearing loss resulting from dead nerves in the inner ear.

Through our steady readjustment to her life with hearing aids, and the heartbreaking realisation that Lucinda had not heard many of the softly spoken words with which we had reassured her in those first twelve months of life, Mike and I shared the feelings and fears we had about the disability. We talked and talked, and I tried to encourage Mike by recounting how well Lucinda was responding to the 'lessons' she had twice a week with the peripatetic teacher of the deaf. These brief 'lessons' were initially more for my benefit than my daughter's; the thinking behind them was that I must know how to help Lucinda. As she would not learn to speak properly from an hour or so here and there it was something Mike and I must work on constantly. The result of our efforts was sheer joy to watch, and it drew us together. After the several weeks of mourning for the loss of Lucinda's normality – there is no other way to phrase it – we were both enormously helped by having something to do, even if it was repeating over and over again 'The airyplanes are up in the sky! . . . eventually Lucinda said 'The ayplanes are up i did i sky'. We hugged her and clapped madly.

When she first wore her aids Lucinda noticed voices, and she was thrilled by the variety of sounds around her. Birds, lorries, television – the excitement of the world was freshly brought to life for her. As things were opening up for her, our disappointment in the face of her problem forced us to communicate and interact as we had not done before and we opened up to each other.

I suppose I had thought that by adding one or two children to one's home a family would be born. Yet it was only now, bewildering though the circumstances appeared, that we were slowly becoming a family. Individuals who were, nonetheless, inter-dependent. Mike and I found ourselves together wanting to create for her the kind of home that was so filled with God's love that she would be enabled to grow up without suffering the isolation of unnecessary misunderstanding and separation from others through her deafness.

She was, and continues to be, an outgoing and courageous inspiration to us both. In the hurly-burly of family squabbles, if someone needs to say sorry, Lucinda is often the first to climb out of herself and bridge any chasm. She has a generous and loving spirit.

Chapter 6

Kate 'at risk' – from whom?

Katharine Amanda Louise arrived on 30 January 1980, a lively, lovable, healthy baby. As Katie is only fourteen and a half months younger than Lucinda their stories overlap, and our new unity as a family resulting from Lucinda's hearing problems, coincided with an alarming problem concerning Kate.

I was still having to battle on a personal level with my confidence, but it was a spring evening in 1980 when events conspired to undermine totally my confidence as a mother.

That night I was adamant that Kate must be in bed early so I'd have time to spend getting myself ready for once! We were going to the cinema. My resolve weakened when I realised that she had been sick on her nightie. I lifted her out of her bouncer. 'Okay, kid,' I said, 'you can have a bath.' It was impossible to resent her, she was such fun to be with.

We gurgled our way upstairs and she sat astride my hip watching alertly as I got things ready and undressed her. I chatted to her about watching the bubbles, as I picked up the soap, wetted it and then slid it back and forth along the groove between her chin and chest. It made her giggle quite infectiously. I marvelled at Kate's ability to enter into life with this hearty abandon at three months old.

We were actively involved in this intimate game when I noticed her right arm. It struck me initially that she had got a lot chubbier recently. Then I sat her up straighter, and realised that the arm was not just fatter, the whole arm was a funny shape. In comparison with the other arm, it did not belong to the same child.

I panicked. So much so, I frightened myself. I took her out of the bath water and, wrapping her in a large warm towel, I ran to the top of the stairs and yelled for Mike. When he did not come immediately, I put a hand over one of Kate's ears and screamed and shouted as loudly as I could, and this time he came, with a look of disbelief! In the eight years he had known me, he had never seen anything like this reaction. I demonstrated that the arm was completely swollen and unrecognisable. Mike, normally the panicker, took firm hold of the situation and the baby, while I went downstairs to confront Sarah, my mother's help.

With no time to collect my thoughts, I simply told her that Kate had a swollen arm, and asked if she had any idea of the cause. I explained that if she remembered dropping her, or seeing Lucinda doing anything which might have been dangerous for such a tiny baby, it would help to know, because the arm looked so peculiar and my mind was inventing all manner of rare diseases. Sarah, who had not yet seen it, could not offer any suggestions . . . and seemed almost unmoved, while I stood there trembling from the shock of seeing that elephantine limb.

I tore upstairs again and cautiously lifted the baby from her Daddy's arms, nervous of hurting her. I could hear Sarah and Lucinda slowly making their way to the bathroom as Mike got through to our doctor. I was very relieved to hear that he could come round directly.

After a short examination, the doctor ruled out bites and stings, and sat down to write a note for the hospital. Within twenty minutes we had started the car and Mike, Kate and I were driving up the road to the nearest casualty department.

There was not a long queue, and we were almost immediately shown into a cubicle, where we waited while various people poked their heads through the curtains. Some had specific jobs to do like taking Kate's temperature and getting us to fill in forms. Others just wanted to meet Kate who, despite the late hour, was rising to the occasion . . . grinning at everyone and with a genuine sparkle in her eyes!

Mike and I went over and over whether I had noticed anything odd about her that morning when I dressed her. To begin with I was categorically certain there had been nothing amiss. Then, as the minutes ticked by and we both became more anxious, and still no one appeared to co-ordinate or explain what was happening, I began questioning everything. Such are the mind's tricks, I could not even be sure of getting her dressed at all that morning!

We were finally told to go up to the X-ray department. Kate did not like being held down so that her arm was still for the picture. But at least we felt we were getting somewhere, and finally the orthopaedic consultant on call came into casualty at about 10 pm to interpret the film.

It was quite a disappointment after such a long wait to be told that it was not clear enough, and that another X-ray would be needed. So we felt pretty jaded by the time we all stood round for a second time to stare at the X-ray which was finally clipped up and lit at about five past eleven. The consultant showed us that Kate had a broken arm, and indicated the point of the break, just above the right elbow. I knew very little about babies' bones except what I had overheard other people say about the extraordinary ability of small children to fall downstairs and suffer no worse than a few bruises because young bones are more rubbery than an adult's.

The shock began to sink in as he told us that babies hardly ever get broken bones, if anything they have what are known as 'greenstick fractures'. But this was not only a real break, it was likely to have happened between one and two weeks ago. 'Do you see this thickening?' He pointed with his index finger. 'The break has already begun to mend.' I gaped at him, feeling violated, deeply hurt that Kate could have lived through something so awful without my sharing it with her. What an ineffectual mother I was . . . failing to offer comfort in her pain. I thought of the daily routine – getting dressed and undressed, stuffing that damaged arm through the sleeves of vests and cardigans, with little more thought than if it had belonged to Suzie, Lucinda's favourite doll. I was dumbfounded, and couldn't help thinking, 'What must this chap think of me?'

'How has she been in herself?' he asked, ignoring the 'conversation' Katie was carrying on with one of the nurses as she snuggled into my shoulder. Now I had seen both swelling and X-ray I hardly knew how to reply . . . what possible relevance could my insensitive observation have? 'She has been much the same as usual', I said. 'She doesn't sleep much during the day, but she never has done, so I have ceased worrying about that; she enjoys being awake and just gurgles and looks around her.' I paused to look at Mike. Had he any ideas? Then I did remember something. 'She did wake two or three nights running earlier this week. I assumed it was her teeth, she's getting them terribly young, or else that she might have wind. So each time I took her downstairs to the kitchen for a cuddle and some gripe water. Once, I think, she had Calpol because she seemed so hot and bothered. But on each occasion she settled again within minutes.'

It was nearly midnight by the time Kate's little arm had been plastered. She fell asleep, utterly exhausted. We were being allowed home with her for the night, to pack a bag, but they wanted us to be admitted to the children's ward the following morning, to keep Kate under observation and do a number of tests.

As we drove home, I looked down at the peaceful, sleeping face.

I felt very low. I had heard vaguely of 'brittle bone disease' and was fearful of that prospect. I was in fact disorientated. To think that we had been looking forward to seeing a good film – I still had the tickets in my pocket . . . and now this. Kate's tiny body was completely dominated by the bulk of the plaster. Whatever I did, I could not satisfy myself that I was holding her comfortably. Either her arm was supported but I imagined the plaster must be cutting into her upper arm, or I let it hang naturally, in which case the weight dragged the entire shoulder down with it.

I put her gently into her cot as soon as we got home and went downstairs to make Mike and myself some hot chocolate. When I accidentally let the milk boil over, I roared at it, giving vent to some of my anger and frustration. I felt helpless, and though nothing had been said, a finger pointed accusingly at me.

Instead of sleeping that night, I tossed and turned, half listening for her to wake. Annoyed that she did not, I slept fitfully . . . it seemed wrong that we were not together, I needed to be with her even if she did not call for me.

Eventually it was 6.30 am and the sun began to pour through our bedroom windows. I felt tired, but less depressed than I had been before dawn. I didn't feel like going back to sleep, so Mike and I talked for nearly an hour. Unwilling to waken properly at such a time on a Sunday, he mumbled at me, his head buried under the pillow. We were both flummoxed by a total lack of explanations for the break. The culprit could have been an ill-fitting pram seat which rested on top of the pram, to enable Lucinda to go out with Kate. It made me shudder to think that it could have slid back and clonked Kate's upper arm. Mike and I couldn't come to a conclusion because when she was outside in the cold Kate was always wrapped in several thick blankets . . . but in the absence of any alternative we decided to mention this to the hospital staff. (When we did, the suggestion was discounted.)

We didn't reach the hospital until about midday by the time I had prepared lunch for the others and packed for Kate and me. As we climbed the stairs to the Children's Wing, I carried Kate, and Mike took my old suitcase.

Unlike the glossy paint and modern planning of the main hospital, these wards appeared makeshift. We were led into a ward with about three beds and as many cots. There were paintings and collages all over the walls, and a pile of soft toys the length of the far window sill. But the children and their parents who had come visiting looked bored, and I felt estranged. My impression was not helped by a little Asian boy in the cot next to Kate's, who seemed very frightened and alone. Everyone was ignoring him and as his crying grew louder it became almost threatening, a weird wailing noise, sending shivers down my spine. I wondered what on earth we were doing bringing wide-eyed, happy Katie into this extraordinarily unthera-peutic place.

I held Kate very close to me and whispered to her that it was lunchtime. I quietly undid the buttons on my shirt, and as discreetly as I could, began feeding her. Her trust and contentment proved too much for me. It was the very antithesis of the mournful crying and depressing aura in the room. I just sat there while great big, wet tears spilled over and soaked the tiny hand which caressed my skin. The worst part was not so much having to look after her arm, but the waiting while doctors, radiologists and laboratory researchers completed their tests.

We spent four to five days there, Kate in a cot in a small side room, and me sleeping on a Z-bed, looking after her as well as taking every opportunity to go home and check that Sarah and Lucinda had all they needed. The laboratory came up with nothing. There was no indication of bone disease or infection, neither did subsequent X-rays tell me anything, so Mike and I were forced to stifle intellectual inquiry, and take Kate home, no further on in solving the mystery.

The first night we were all together again, I gave Lucinda a bit of extra attention and we read several picture books before we had a cuddle . . . a vital part of instilling confidence and security for her. I sat in thought about the whole episode until she began drifting into sleep, when I crept out of the room. I had to ask

Sarah once more if there was anything she hadn't told me, since there was something in her attitude that bothered me.

I stood by the fire in the drawing room while she perched on the arm of the sofa, 'I see from my diary that you had Kate one afternoon nearly three weeks ago. Do you remember taking her to tea at little Philip's house? Sarah, I realise that this is difficult for you, but it is so important that you try to recall any incident, however insignificant it may have appeared at the time. Is there anything that happened either during the course of that afternoon, or at any other time, which you have not told me about? I shan't be cross, only relieved to have some kind of answer to all the questions which still crowd into my mind. Is there anything?'

'No, there isn't, honestly,' she said, immediately.

'Are you sure?'

'Yes quite sure, I promise,' came her final reply.

'Right, let's forget it' I said.

That was the last time any of us intended to bring up the subject. We ate supper that night in front of the television. There was a mutual, if unspoken, resolve between Mike and myself to put the whole thing behind us and get on with life. We laughed more that evening than we had during the whole of the previous fortnight.

Mike and I had found ourselves leaning on each other as a result of these recent events. It left me feeling terribly in love with him and uncharacteristically dependent! The experience of being incarcerated in that hospital found me more appreciative of our lovely home and of the freedom to move around. I was content. Then, only ten days later, I was climbing into bed with the Sunday papers when the telephone rang. I was frankly startled to hear the consultant paediatrician on the line at ten fifteen at night!

His tone precluded small talk. He wanted me to get Mike to the telephone, so I ran downstairs and asked him to go to the extension in the dining room. Then tore back to my bedroom. My stomach was churning. I had an awful feeling that he must have rung to tell us about a particular culture which had been maturing in the laboratory. Was Kate suffering from some rare and ghastly disease?

What he did say was so unexpected, it was like being poised ready for a blow in the chest, only to be knocked unconscious from behind. He had rung because the Social Services had discovered, from a hospital employee, that Kate had a broken arm that was unaccounted for, and they were placing her name on the 'At Risk Register'. Mike asked him to enlarge. I think I had by then heard of the term but neither of us knew the implications of it. I felt sick as he explained that two entries on the register could result in the children of that family being taken 'into care'.

'Lissa,' he said kindly, 'you are bound find it unnerving dealing with critical, unwanted visitors and I would like to help you work out how you are going to handle the situation when the CID, social workers and NSPCC decide to call. It would be unwise for you to put anyone's back up, so I want you both to be fully acquainted with the facts as they are. Can we meet on Tuesday.'

It was agreed, and when the conversation ended, Mike and I met face to face saying nothing . . . there was nothing to say.

This knowledge that I was now on an official list of 'dangerous' mothers outraged as well as hurt me. I would have to busy myself, right away. It was time for Katie's evening top-up, so I went straight into her room and switched on the lamp. Kate was in a deep sleep, oblivious of me pensively taking in little details of the room. So many things reminded me of my childhood, Beatrix Potter ornaments, fresh white paint and a wicker-work chair. In such a place security and love is engendered.

I took a deep breath and lifted her carefully from her cot. I looked at the eyelashes curving away from her cheeks, and she smiled, enjoying a happy dream. Then I glanced quickly at the splint on her arm which had been firmly secured for the night, before allowing my eyes to settle again on that peaceful face. What a fool I was to be affected by what other people thought of me. I unfastened my nightie, and she fed . . . half-heartedly, benefiting more from the cuddle than the milk, and then dozed off again.

I was leaning over her about to change her nappy when I realised that I was not in fact a stong enough person to cope with some people thinking I had battered Kate. Suddenly it got right to me, and broke down my confidence so swiftly that I felt I could not touch her. If I was accused of hurting Kate maybe the world had lost all reason and anything could happen.

Mike came into the room and found me, round-shouldered and sobbing uncontrollably. He gave me a look which meant 'Not much point in changing that nappy tonight,' and he laid Kate down again. We went to bed, I held Mike's hand . . . I was broken.

The next morning I was still shaken and went to walk by the Thames for an hour or more. There was no point in my being at home, I could not yet handle Kate at all. I wore the heaviness of grieving for a seal of motherhood that seemed no longer mine.

I decided that being misunderstood was unfathomable,

because if someone misunderstands you at all, there is no knowing exactly how far removed from the truth their impression is. I began to wonder how Jesus had handled being misunderstood; not so much the failure of so many people to grasp why He had come, and what He was doing . . . but the everyday, human feeling of being out on a limb. Gradually out of my bewilderment the idea took hold that only God could understand how I felt and I experienced an almost physical sense of His arms around me. I had no idea what was happening in my life, but I knew that things were beyond my control. For once there was nothing I could do, He was inviting me to accept His love, and His strength.

We kept our appointment with the consultant the following afternoon, when he explained that Kate must have been handled very roughly indeed to have sustained not only the break, but two soft tissue injuries, one above the break and a second on the opposite ankle. These had been picked up on the later X-rays. He talked with us at great length, and subsequently interviewed Sarah too.

It was four weeks later that I said 'Hello, come this way' as I opened the front door to a casually dressed, bearded man in his mid-thirties. 'So this is our Social Services Representative,' I thought. As we walked into the drawing room I motioned to a chair, he sat down and I began directly.

'Our other daughter is in hospital . . . she had a barium enema only this afternoon so I've had a rush getting here, I didn't want to leave her until she had settled,' I explained. 'And in case you're wondering, it is the strain of Kate's condition, or rather your "interest" in her welfare, coupled with Lucinda's illness which have combined to give me a kind of physical breakdown. That's why I'm wearing this collar because of the pain in my back. Katie, as you can see, is the only one of us looking well – she has been spending a good deal of her time "at risk" in her pram gaining a healthy suntan.' I hadn't intended to be so rude, but I was angry. From across the room there was no response, so I went on talking nervously searching for reactions from him which would help me to get the measure of him. In fact all he told me was that a Case Conference of eight people had met the previous month for one and a half hours. Nobody had represented us, which made my blood boil. Mike, as usual, spoke far less than me, but asked all the vital questions. The Social Services man spent fifteen minutes or so reiterating what the consultant had illustrated at our meeting with him. Taking all the X-rays into account, there was clear evidence of complications: the two soft tissue injuries meant that Katie's injury was not consistent with a knock or fall, but that she must have been handled very roughly to have sustained such injuries. We told him that knowing about the sprains had made it no easier for us to find an explanation for them. He asked me if anyone else had handled Kate other than myself, 'Not really', I said 'She's been pretty unresponsive to Sarah so I look after her most of the time, although she did go with Sarah to a tea party a few weeks ago.'

This first interview continued while I fed Kate and we ascertained the full facts about the At Risk Register. Kate's name would be deleted from the list in December if neither she nor her sister suffered injury in the meantime. There would be no way that we could get access to it to check that she had been taken off the list, – we would have to take his word for it. I had to break in at that point, Lucinda had only been walking a few months. 'Look,' I said, 'I fully understand that you need to protect some children, but you can't mean to tell me that if Lucinda has a fall or accidentally hurts Kate, either of which is quite likely, you will take them away from us!'

'That is the way it works' he said, 'but we would obviously take into consideration those accidents which had clearly resulted from childhood play.' We parted after an hour or more, Mike and I feeling even more threatened but also relieved that this dreaded visit was over. We would apparently be notified of the next one in a couple of months.

Mike and I avoided talking openly about this to more than a very few people. I feared that if the neighbours knew the suspicion under which I was held, I would start imagining the law coming to take me away every time one of the children cried. As it was we had a visit from two CID inspectors one evening, the health visitor came weekly instead of monthly and our friendly social services man came twice more.

This trauma had so turned my life upside down, that I found myself getting down to basics, other things seeming irrelevant and unimportant. I had unexpectedly put a huge question mark over everything . . . I even found myself wondering whether I was depressed any more, or whether it had become a habit, for me to think of myself as a hopeless case. This was all new. The introspection was unlike all former self-doubt, instead of finding nothing but my failings I was able to stand outside myself and see a little of what I was really like without either exaggeration or false modesty. Not only was I sustaining a good relationship with each of my children but Mike and I had grown closer as we talked our way through the first two difficult months. There was a sense in which I had not run away. With nowhere to turn I had to face up to things, stand firm and be patient. I was surprised and encouraged to discover that I did possess such character traits.

The support which the consultant and our family doctor gave me achieved two results. It boosted my confidence and challenged me to believe that their assessment of me as a mother was not unfounded. Faced with the suspicion of my having harmed Katie, to my mind by far the most damaging lie concerning my life, I actually scorned the perpetual fibs I told about how hungry I was or was not. I found I liked this new determination for honesty. Truth was worth pursuing as an end in itself. It gave me a good feeling. Mercifully there were no more accidents, so that Kate's name eventually came off the Register.

As I began to feel happier in myself, my time was more constructively occupied and I regained some of my inherited optimism. Even cooking became creative, instead of being a drudge. Sarah and I loved to cook but rarely found the time to get down to a really good mess in the kitchen. Consequently one day a week was set aside for stocking the freezer. We would make our staple diet – steak and kidney, fish pie, spaghetti bolognese sauce and quiches – and anything else we specially wanted to try.

Sarah had just finished making some biscuits and my hands were deep in the bowl of crumble mixture. Having only recently discovered Lucinda's hearing loss, I was more than usually sensitive to the atmospheres and surroundings where she went. So I asked, 'Will your parents be at home on Saturday when you take the children to your house?'

'I don't think my dad will, because he's supposed to be working this weekend,' Sarah said.

'The wedding we're going to is quite a long way away –

will you be all right, because we will be back quite late?'

'Yes, my mum will be there, we'll be fine.'

I had heard a lot about her mother but we had only met briefly once and I wanted to know a bit more.

'Does your mother ever go to church?' I said.

'Yes, you know, I told you.'

'No, you never have, – where does she go?' I went on.

'Oh, she goes all the time to that Spiritualist Church round the corner from us . . . she thinks it's marvellous.'

For a moment I was stunned. Most certainly she had *not* told me that before.

'Sarah, has your mother ever talked to you about . . . her faith?'

'Not much, but she says it's very interesting.'

'Anything you can tell me about it or what she does?'

'I've only been once so I couldn't really say, but I did once catch her downstairs in the night and in the morning she told me she had been talking to my Gran.'

'Your Gran?' I felt very uneasy now.

'Yes. She died about three years ago and Mum had always been very close to her . . . and, well, that's about it,' she said.

'Oh,' I said, slowly. 'I see.'

I knew there was a verse in the Bible which said '. . . don't let them consult the spirits of the dead' but I had not given much thought to why not. Faced with this new information, I needed to get outside and to think, alone.

'I'll do this later if I have a minute,' I said. 'It's so lovely out today, do you mind if I pop into the park for half an hour before lunch?'

I washed the flour and margarine off my hands, and grabbing a jacket from the hall, closed the front door quietly behind me. Then I half walked, half ran, until I was through the park gates. When I started to feel calmer I slumped on a bench and wrestled with the thoughts that were coming at me.

It seemed remarkable that I, who had been living such an ineffectual Christian life, and Mike, who had always found it difficult to stand up and be counted should be faced with this situation. We, of all people. Apart from my having been 'filled with the Spirit' some years before we had had no real involvement with the more spiritual side of Christian things . . . I, for my part, was even nervous of getting together in groups to pray – though I tried not to let that show! As I sat there, looking across at the boathouses, I wondered where that Old Testament verse left us. We were not on the fence – we were committed Christians, and we were housing a girl whose mother was involved in something God had specifically said we must never do. I had always understood that verse to be warning us not to interfere with or harm the dead themselves. Yet here was another inference, if Sarah was unwittingly involved . . . perhaps we could be endangered through this connection? I had learnt the short passage when I'd been an eager, new Christian and I knew that it went on, 'The Lord your God hates people who do these disgusting things' ending with, 'Be completely faithful to the Lord.'*

I knew that God had brought us to this crossroads. We were being forced to make a choice, either to take seriously God's anger and His demands upon our loyalty, or to deny the spiritual struggle in which the Bible says the whole world is engaged. I looked at my watch. If I hurried I might just catch Mike before he went out to lunch. I *had* to talk to him. I ran through the park and panted up the street. When I reached the

* Deuteronomy 18:12-13.

house I turned the key, leaving it in the door in my hurry to get to the phone. I could hear Sarah upstairs waking the children up.

I was relieved when Mike answered his line. He listened to what I had to say and then paused for several seconds. There was a quiet confidence in his voice as he replied.

'Sarah must go. It's as simple as that. We will pay her for the whole of this week, and for another full calendar month, but she must not be in our house any longer. I suspect she is completely unaware of what has been happening, but as you know I have often felt that we were being . . . persecuted. Her innocence is not our major concern, our responsibility is to the children and our life together. I think you should consider from whom we should get some advice. I must go, I've got a meeting now. See you tonight.'

He had confirmed everything that I had thought, and I found that especially reassuring.

As the girls, Sarah and myself sat round the kitchen table for lunch, I realised that as God is all-loving He must have a plan for her too. So I prayed 'Please Lord, surround Sarah when I talk to her. Protect her from the pain of rejection . . . I don't want to hurt her . . . but this is rather beyond me: if I do what we feel you want, please will you take care of her?'

That night, when we could be alone, I spoke to Sarah. Putting it simply, I told her she had been a wonderful help. I had grown fond of her and the children would miss her, but as Christians, we could not go on employing her because of her family's Spiritualist connection. I had expected her to react to that quite strongly but when she didn't I said that I would be happy to give her a reference if she decided to work for another family, as long as they were not in the front line of a spiritual battle. At that point Mike joined us.

We then talked together for a quarter of an hour, and during that time she showed no recognisable response, and voiced none of the things I had expected like 'Funny kind of love, Christian love is, turning me out on the street with only a few minutes warning!' I looked for signs that she was suppressing deep hurt and anger, but I could not detect anything . . . it was as if she had no personality of her own at all. Within the hour we said our goodbyes and she drove off with her father.

The next morning I was in quite a state and impatient to get advice about what, if anything, we should do. I rang Audrey, someone older than myself who had been a Christian for many years. She promised to contact David, a mutual friend, who had also been instrumental in my conversion at Oxford in 1970. When he arrived, as planned, the following evening, Mike and I were very humbled to think that he should have interrupted an overloaded schedule to travel all the way from Birmingham to London to help us.

We welcomed him and then sat down to a simple supper in the kitchen. I had been feeling anxious, extraordinarily anxious, ever since hearing that Sarah's mother was involved with the spirit world, and I had been dreading the evening, not knowing what to expect.

Yet as the three of us talked and David shared some of his own experiences, it seemed an entirely natural progession to ask God to banish whatever was unwanted in our home and to fill it instead with His presence and His love.

Mike described the period since Sarah had come to live in our home. Apart from Kate's broken arm, Lucinda's eight days in hospital with a gastric disorder, two and a half days of which were spent on a glucose drip, one of us had had either a cold or a stomach upset *every* weekend that year. It was pow-pow-pow! The day after Sarah arrived I began to bleed and was confined to bed in case I lost baby Kate, and from then on it was a remarkable catalogue of disasters, they came one after the other, wearing us out and apparently timed to affect body blows when we were already down. After that my back had become so acutely painful and I had only just thrown away my orthopaedic collar when we were faced with adjusting to Lucinda's hearing difficulty. Mike admitted that there something weird and yet ludicrous about it all.

Now in the kitchen there was humour, warmth and a remarkable normality about David's conversation. He confirmed that it was important to take any spiritual struggle seriously, reminding us of Ephesians 6:12 'For we are not fighting against human beings but against the wicked spiritual forces in the heavenly world . . .' But pausing to dwell on that, David took great care to explain that, as Christians, we must rely on what Jesus has already done. He said that although we do not know exactly what happened when Jesus was on the cross, He did something to destroy the power of Satan, so that all we needed to do was to take authority over any evil spirit in the name of Jesus, because He has complete authority over the spirit world.

When the doorbell went, Mike got up to let Audrey in. She joined us while David explained how often the devil attempts to influence our lives. In our case he had found the weakest spot – the area about which we rarely communicated – illness, and just worked away at it until we became completely vulnerable. Mike remembered that he had commented a number of times during the year on the alarming regularity with which things kept going wrong. He now said 'We knew it was odd, but most of the time we were too tired and too shell-shocked to take stock.'

We moved through into the drawing room where David prayed and I was reminded of God's promise that if we are agreed, whatever we asked will be done for us. I can't speak for Mike, but I felt out of my depth or should I say, unable to contribute, although there was nothing alarming or eerie about the manner in which the other two prayed.

We went round the house, and either David or Audrey prayed in the name of Jesus for us to be able to use each room, to be free to know the presence of God wherever we were in our home, and I found it particularly reassuring to pray in each of the children's rooms, as they slept, claiming for them the protection that God provided for them as His children.

It was not until we reached the room where Sarah had slept, that they sensed something which they had not felt elsewhere. I kept my eyes closed as David's voice became more commanding in tone, taking authority, in the name of Jesus, over an evil spirit and those influences which had got in to our home and lives to such damaging effect. He reminded us that Jesus had removed our guilt by his drastic measure of dying for us and he clarified for us that as we were guilt-free, no evil could now take hold of us and limit us. Then he paused to confirm to us that he also believed Sarah to be an innocent channel, unaware of what had been accomplished through her by the evil spirit. I felt . . .freed.

Not knowing what to expect from David's visit, I had certainly not anticipated the wonderful sense of both security and freedom with which God surrounded us.

When we found ourselves alone, as we got ready for bed, we were aware that God had altered our attitude. I could remember having read 1 Corinthians 2:5 'Your faith, then, does not rest on human wisdom but on God's power'. This very night God had shown us that despite our inclination to self-sufficiency, ultimately *in everything*, even for our protection we *needed God's power*. We now trusted Him and were left with an enduring gratitude to Him and to the unselfish friend who had travelled so far in one evening to help us close that unforgettable chapter in our lives.

Chapter 7

'Our heaven is now, is won!'

Breathless, we flung us on the windy hill,
Laughed in the sun and kissed the lovely grass . . .
'Heart of my heart our heaven is now, is won!'

So from that extraordinary year of 1980, we came in the springtime of 1981, not upon a hill in the burgeoning English countryside, like Rupert Brooke, but to an island called Penang with a hill where the first funicular railway was built, and copious sandy beaches. And to an unprecedented enjoyment of each other. Closer to God, I was finding an enthusiasm and urgency to repair other relationships.

Mike had done some business in Hong Kong, where we spent ten days with friends – now we had six and a half days remaining for ourselves. This was our first opportunity, since either of the children were born, to be together and realise how far our love had come and had deepened as a result of enduring long desert experiences.

It was towards evening on our first day, as a breeze picked up, that I walked along the sand. It was cooler at this hour to the soles of my feet. I was overwhelmed by the beauty of the place. A great fireball sun was sinking slowly behind the sea; I could not remember actually having seen it as it fell before. Finally it disappeared in the right angle between the wide horizon and the rocky promontory which formed the outpost of our bay.

I had already evolved a daily habit of turning my thoughts God-ward, but the sky on that night highlighted and confirmed the glory of Heaven. The past few months had provided a plateau, and once God got me up on to it I had felt Him saying to me, 'In these past years I have been talking to you, don't doubt that, but you have failed to listen. I am not going to lose this opportunity to speak to you now that you are receptive to me.'

Ever since leaving Heathrow it had been as though the Lord was digging me in the ribs and saying, 'What about Mike?' After one fun day on a junk with a crowd of friends I'd sat down, my Bible open on my lap . . . and the hint had come back, 'What about Mike?' That week I stopped separating the spiritual from the rest of my world . . . God showed me that He had planned the best for us, that He cared about the whole of my life and he wanted it to be abundantly full. The trouble was that I found it easier to be close to Him by having an overtly 'spiritual' time each day . . . than to appropriate His healing and energy to my bruised marriage.

Standing alone, I was aware that over the years I had been the unresponsive one, often thinking that God had 'made a mistake' in bringing us together. On that beach I promised God that I was now ready for Him to bring us together as He had planned. I was frustrated – wanting more in our marriage relationship. So it was half an acknowledgement of my willingness and half a challenge to God: 'Okay, if we are right together, show me the truth of that. What *about* Mike?' If I give myself – can you please make it something *good*?'

As the week drew to a close, with a wry smile, I remembered praying that 'cheeky' prayer! 'We *do* speak the same language, Lord – you have my best interests at heart.' Why had I doubted it? In those days on the water, in the hot sun and the cool of the air-conditioning, we had learned to say sorry for what had been unsaid, as much as for what had been said to hurt. They were days of the sheer abandonment of love, God's gift to us both. Each other and our bodies in His healing of our minds.

When I first started roughly planning this book, thinking about this chapter, I wrote: 'There is something about being taken beyond one's limit of endurance – even one step back from the edge of a cliff seems like safety and security.'

That sums up what I felt in the autumn of 1980. Six great months were then sandwiched between my acknowledgement of that feeling and our holiday in the Far East. They were months of learning and finding freedom.

A few feet away from the edge, I found not only answers, but questions, flooding my brain. My prison of introspection and self-doubt was no longer inviolable. I tentatively opened up and found I liked what was happening.

I wrote in a diary:

> Who am I? What or which role(s) am I here to play in this vast and confusing world? I can only know the answer to that by asking, and not once for all time, but again and again
> Please God – who am I?
> Because, Lord Jesus, I am different today as a result

of things which happened yesterday, and today's agenda is not a bit like tomorrow's. For me, as for other women, there are opportunities as never before – but I can't make use of them. I don't even cope from day to day. Help me not to strive or to thrust myself forward. The 'world' is thrusting, pushing, relentless, but instead, help me to lie back as you invite me to.

That unexpurgated quotation shows me how far I had come from those feelings of nothingness I had had only a year or two before. The question 'Who am I?' was healthy evidence that at last I wanted a reply . . . there was a gleam of light at the end of the long dark tunnel, which I had glimpsed the night our home was cleansed, and Mike and I had been freed from the weight of so many calamities.

Invigorated, like a bird learning to fly, I made 'sorties' during those months. Some more successful than others. But there was no going back again to the limiting confines of the nest. My eating habits had radically improved over the past year. Lasting often two and maybe three months without being sick, when I did fall to the ground it hurt. The degradation and squalor of such behaviour were the more revolting the nearer I got to normality. Now I was taking a long objective look at my lifestyle, and was prepared to alter anything if it would speed my recovery.

Going through my wardrobe I decided that most of my clothes were too tight! So one sunny morning I leapt on the bus and made for Sloane Square where I purchased a buttercup yellow tracksuit in Peter Jones. The loose-fitting casual garment epitomised my new attitude. I had determined to unlearn calculated perfection, and make spontaneity my goal.

In October, I began reading Psalm 139 regularly, like

one brushes one's teeth! Some days I would read the whole thing, and on others I scribbled down one or two verses and kept them in my pocket, or pinned them to the notice board in the kitchen. I referred to them at odd times, checking the effect they had as much when I felt low as when things were going well. So my 'thing' that autumn became turning my back on how I had seen myself in the past. I was no longer going to starve my body into submission. It had rights too! If it needed a broader profile, and looser fitting, more comfortable clothes I must alter my mind's messages. So I allowed the words of the Psalm to penetrate my life. To repair my mind and to restore those areas of my body that I had for so long ignored and loathed. I read,

> 'Lord . . . you know me. You know everything I do; from far away you understand all my thoughts. You see me, whether I am working or resting; you know all my actions. . . . Your knowledge of me is too deep; it is beyond understanding.'

Often I would cry at that point. Wherever I was, in a traffic jam, in the supermarket or at home . . . they went so deep. I needed a lot of time to assimilate them.

The *Living Bible* brought certain verses alive even more:

> I can never get away from my God! If I go up to heaven, you are there; if I go down to the place of the dead, you are there . . . You made all the delicate inner parts of my body, and knit them together in my mother's womb. Thank you for making me so wonderfully complex! . . . You were there while I was being formed in utter seclusion. You saw me before I

> was born and scheduled each day of my life before I began to breathe . . . How precious it is Lord to realise that you are thinking about me constantly . . . when I waken in the morning, you are still thinking of me!

But although most of me was longing to accept all of that I was still bothered by the idea of God thinking of me all the time. There was a struggle between the helpless me, which longed for that to be true, and the independent personality which told itself that I was coping with my problems myself and that it would be downright presumptive of me to think that a busy God would bother with my little life. I had been accustomed to doing my bit, and I could not quite believe that God loved me unless I had done something to warrant it.

Something marvellous was happening though. And I wrote, somewhat bravely I think, looking back at it, 'God loves what is me. I must go on saying that until I believe it. And I must find a way to love it too.' I bubbled over each evening dying to tell Mike about the little encouragements that were making such a big difference in my life. I think most of the time he thought me quite mad. Gradually I found I could look in a mirror and see myself as I in fact was . . . which was only what Mike had always seen! Brave enough to be objective, I was not mentally adding two or three inches to motivate myself to slim a bit more. But I could not begin to convey the excitement of that to him. However, we both enjoyed a revival of my sense of humour – able to laugh at myself once again, Mike and I stole mid-night hours to giggle and talk. For me it was a coming back to each other.

Yet there was a menacing cloud which continued to

hang over me. Whenever I took two steps forward I found myself taking another one back. Bulimia Nervosa prevented my finding 'the peace which passes all understanding.' Then ironically the first experience I had of real peace came from the exposure of my secret habit.

It was a Saturday afternoon. Mike and I were at home, having finished lunch, and I had spent the past twenty minutes, instead of clearing up, eating the left-overs. Now I stood poised over the spotless lavatory bowl, my heart pounding. 'I must get rid of this bulk or I shan't get through the day,' I was muttering.

Suddenly Mike's voice shouted up the stairs, 'Come on, it's going to rain later, let's go and have a walk!' I didn't answer . . . I just froze. 'What are you doing?' he asked. He sounded annoyed because I guess he knew full well – my behaviour had been transparently erratic that morning.

Then I heard his foot on the stairs and I realised that this was *it* . . . my nightmare, what I had lived in dread of for the past eight years. What could I do? Nothing.

The next thing I remember was a command; 'Open the door'. Which I did, turning back immediately to look at the cistern. 'This is hell' I remember thinking. He stood behind me and I felt his hands on my shoulders. Sparing me the degradation of having to look him in the face. He gently leaned me back on his chest, my shoulders tense and quivering, his kind normality throwing my alienation and sluttishness into sharper contrast, and his voice remained firm and steady, 'I mean it, it is a beautiful afternoon, and you're coming with me . . . and that's final'. 'I *can't*' I blurted out. 'But can't you see, I can't. I *must* be sick. You don't understand, I know, but I have no option, I never do, and now I've eaten this much I have to be sick or I shall burst.'

Mike remained intransigent. He'd known about this business for some years now, but had never caught me in the act. He led me downstairs, holding my arm firmly as I was trying to get away from him. Whining and shaking, I was short of breath and aching from the distended stomach. But he was forcing me, with gentleness, to go 'cold turkey', missing out on the 'fix' of vomiting.

We walked and walked, me unwillingly at first, like a rebellious child. But after four miles I began to feel that I would survive the ordeal. After five I could hardly believe I still had my skin round all that food. But I was beginning to feel like other people. And when I finally opened my mouth to speak it was to say, 'Some people, no, most people, overeat sometimes, don't they?' Mike nodded and we walked on in silence. As we covered the final hundred yards or so back to the front gate, the trembling and palpitations had stopped. I was 'full to bursting' and likely to feel that way for some time . . . but, interestingly, I managed to get on with clearing up the lunch . . . and without even a thought of eating more.

By loving me when, God knows how unlovable I was, Mike had introduced me to the adult concept of taking responsibility for one's actions. By accepting me at that moment when the bottom fell out of my world, he had shown me an alternative, a way out, and I had experienced peace where there had always been trauma and disgust. In preventing me from walking away, I could at last look myself in the face. There was now a real hope of change.

So encouraged by that staggering fact which I repeated

to myself 'The other afternoon *I was not sick*,' I decided to look for those steps which God already knew I had to take in order to beat this thing. I did not arrange to see any counsellors in the immediate future, which helped me turn another corner. Having for so long rushed off to someone else for their help, I was inquisitive to know if Jesus could speak directly to me. So I offered Him my willingness, and asked that He might teach me whenever and wherever I needed to learn.

The first opportunity to learn came during a weekend spent with good friends near Newbury. While enjoying tennis and delicious hospitality in their lovely home I found myself scrutinising, I hoped with some tact, exactly what Clare ate. She fascinated me because of her sheer zest for life and the appetite which she always satisfied. And she struck me as being a good model to watch, partly because we were about the same size and height, but also because of her infectious ability to take from fashion, including its obsession with slimming, just exactly what she wanted to, ignoring the rest. Such confidence was refreshing.

On our return to London we had scrambled eggs and then I went in search of the notebook I had kept up for some years. I was hoping to find certain clues, from which I could start. I knew it would be hard work, but I wanted to build something entirely new. A workaday experience of eating according to appetite rather than emotion. I had to go back to the drawing board. Most of my guilt and hurt had been worked through with counsellors. I had often been prayed for, hands had been laid on me and sometimes the Holy Spirit had stepped in by giving a word of wisdom to one of the people praying for me, cutting out the need for endless hours of discussion. Each hurdle crossed had made sense to me and I'd break down, with sheer gratitude for the clarification given.

But as I sat in the armchair in our bedroom, the notebook open, I closed my eyes and quietly asked God to restore my natural likes and dislikes, to continue the healing He had already started on my appetite, and to enable me to stop categorising food and putting pressure on myself to diet. I wanted more now. I wanted to be able to give Him glory for a perfect and complete healing. Then I read the first entry 'If anyone is in Christ he is a new creation, the old has passed away . . .' This had always made me feel such a liar, so inadequate, it had paralysed me . . . now it was as if, were there a time for everything, this was my time to get to grips with this verse. I stood up and reached for my Bible, long closed and gathering dust on my bedside table. While thumbing through to complete the verse I found another in Ephesians '. . . and you must put on the new self'. 'That's it. That's what I need,' I thought. 'I want to be how God wants me to be, even if it is fatter or different in any way – so I can be free to get beyond myself, to reach out to other people and to Him, to forgive, to create and to love.'

So taking this notebook as my basis for further work I read through the discoveries I had made about my eating habits. How I often drank coffee when I was actually hungry, not thirsty. How thirst made me tense and tension made me eat, so that I should learn to recognise my real need: drink or food. My inability to trust myself to impose my own limit to what I ate. A list of the foods, I had discovered that I really liked. That tiredness was a monster with which I could not cope, that I *needed* exercise. Some details were entered neatly and others barely legible, but there was an overall naivety yet also a painstaking conscientiousness. I had simply recorded anything that might possibly fit one day into the jigsaw puzzle.

This whole thing must seem extraordinary to anyone who eats sensibly when their body tells them they are hungry. But the point was that I had *everything* to learn. As I closed the book and hugged my knees to my chin, deep in thought, I could already see that this groundwork would be invaluable. The zombie who lived with limited hope had realised a measure of dignity . . . and Mike ought not to be expected to wait for ever.

It struck me that what I needed was someone with whom I could bounce off ideas and share my progress with. I needed someone who would have some sympathy with behavioural study (which was what I could see it would amount to), and would have an interest in sharing in it on her own account. It had to be someone I trusted – totally. A girl called Joanna, whom I already knew quite well, came immediately to mind. She was not yet a close friend, but I knew she had had experience of God's healing, and her problems were completely different to mine. I reckoned that she would neither pass out with shock when I told her about my 'secret', nor blanch at my rather direct approach and sense of humour. Moreover she lived close-by and only worked part-time, and would be available to me, as I would to her, if either of us got tense or panicky. Could we lean on each other, I wondered?

Most of us can recall crazy moments which we look back on with fondness – they were 'right', one even knew it at the time. I had that sort of feeling the Sunday afternoon I curled up on the floor in front of the fire and began writing to Joanna. Easing my way in with thank yous for a party she and Jonathan had given the night before, then opening up, cautiously, I was soon pouring myself on to the paper.

I told her that I had had so much healing, but that I now felt I was calling God a liar, and the power of His Holy Spirit impotent, if I did not make a better job of living victoriously. It was a very human, earthly letter. I said that I needed someone to help me learn the new behaviour which went with being healed. It was entirely inappropriate now to keep going back for healing, and I had for now got beyond the stage of needing a counsellor. My problem was in getting on with life, whilst the scars of the healing were so lividly in evidence. Would she join me and grapple with the effects of tension in each of our lives? Then we could help each other to recognise our panics for what they were . . . scars, which were a result of healing, not its denial.

I told her that I was pretty frightened of opening up at all unless what we talked about was absolutely confidential, and cautioned her to ask Jonathan if he minded her involvement in such an experiment of mutual support. I suggested we might tell someone else, older and wiser, of what we were doing, in case one of us off-loaded too much on to the other one on an already bad day, and I added that when the tension started to build up, I usually became totally vulnerable, panicking that I had lost control again . . . I knew I was asking a lot of her, it would be no picnic.

The final paragraph allowed room for the free movement of the Holy Spirit.

> Your vision of what I am suggesting may be totally different from mine. If it is, that can only be good. Then we shall bring our individual expectation of

> God's potential to act to every situation. We shall need to be open to each other and to God. If the Holy Spirit is in control I won't need to ring you just at the moment when Jonathan is likely to be getting back from work, neither will one of us overload the other, but we must pray for special sensitivity.

Subconsciously I was looking forward to deepening our friendship too. If one slips into the habit of lying to the extent that I had, one finds oneself lonely. I was thrilled when her enthusiasm for this venture matched mine.

My illness had only become treatable when I had realised that it was related to self-acceptance. Now with Joanna's regular help I was trying to evaluate those situations and emotions which upset me, and to workout how I might avoid them or handle them differently in the future. I had to recognise tension. Recognise anger – learn to express anger rather than suppress it, and work hard on the ongoing thing of linking eating to appetite.

As the weeks passed I added to the scribblings in my notebook the little comments which I believed God was telling me at different times during the week. It filled with odd remarks like 'Don't "pick" out of large serving bowls, always put my helping on to a plate and sit down to enjoy it,' and 'Be positive about what I eat. Take vitamin B for my nerves.' I had to learn to eat enough at meals and walk away from the temptation to slim all the time. Although vomiting gradually became a thing of the past . . . my eating tended to centre around the 'secrecy element' and I still preferred midnight feasts in the kitchen to meals with other people.

In fact the whole subject of learning to eat with other people was a difficult one, and I am sure that there are others who are better qualified and more able to express the social and psychological problems involved. I found it hard to cope with any conversation about eating habits – mine particularly. It was very difficult not to lie. Other people would say, 'Oh look Lissa's on a diet!' And that would stump me. Was I or was I not on a diet? Not really. I was on a whole new discovery.

The most difficult thing was being with other people who I sensed also had an eating foible, even something as simple as cutting out potatoes. Having at one time made it my aim to eat less than everyone else, it took time for me to be able to have a second helping because I was hungry while other people were pushing the food round their plates. I would share all these things and the effect they had had on me when Joanna and I met for lunch or coffee. Our chat was relaxed and the children played excitedly around the house, in either of our homes. They were very good times.

She was patience and love to me, and we laughed about the most trivial achievements like going ten days without standing on the scales. I remember ringing her one morning because Mike and I had invited eight for dinner that night – always a potentially dangerous situation for me, incorporating people and food. There was a mess in the kitchen, a child upstairs with bronchitis, another crying, no nanny and three quarters of a chocolate cake inside me! I wondered what, if anything Joanna could do, I felt really hopeless. Yet we had agreed to ring each other any time either of us got into a panic . . . so I needed to dial her number before I was beyond help.

She was in and answered the phone herself. So I told her all of this, and then she prayed over the phone for clarity of thought and for me to be aware of the presence of God. Afterwards we talked through, and she encouraged me to assess my priorities for the day and settle on what could be left until the following day. I was not sick and ultimately I discovered that the root of the problem was that I did not know what I was going to wear!

Just as on other occasions when the whirlwind of panic started to whip me up with it, I found that as soon as I had attacked the root problem, whatever it might have been, the other things that had worried me sorted themselves out. On that particular night I not only enjoyed the evening, but I did not feel tired. Tiredness was the thing I most dreaded. In fact I frequently made myself tired by panicking that I would be tired! When I rang Joanna again to tell her that I had been okay, she reminded me that all she had done was to listen, and reassure me.

Oddly enough most of my re-programming about food could have been traced back to a remark Mike had once made. We were on holiday, five months after getting married, and I had asked him what he wanted to drink. He had laughed and said, 'I haven't decided, I am still consulting my taste buds!' 'I like that,' I said. 'I'll remember that'.

With Joanna I did remember things like that. Little gems which had never been put to use. I listened to what other people said, watched people in restuarants, and then prayed about whether there was an application to my own life. I discovered that there was a radical difference between wanting a bar of chocolate because I felt like it, and *having* to have a bar, or five or six, because the compulsion was engulfing. I began to reject the noises I could hear in my brain . . . those slimming ads and jingles and the things people said when they were dieting. As Joanna and I dug deep and faced our fears, God put confidence where there had been despair and inadequacy.

I was profoundly moved by this experience of deep committed friendship . . . God used it to lead me away from the years of depression and bulimia nervosa. In those eight months especially, she was indeed an angel of God, and I shall for ever be thankful for her belief in me.

In 1981 I went as far as acknowledging to God and to Joanna that I was healed of the bulimia, but the temptation to re-open the wound and resume that destruction did not leave me until late 1982. I had the approach of a small child – addressing myself 'Dare I believe? It seems too good to be true'.

I survived two memorable evenings alone in the house, when the effort to resist making myself sick brought me out in a terrifying sweat. I gave me a penetrating insight into the dilemma facing drug addicts when they try to break their habit.

At the time I fought against vomiting because I knew that the only way out was to turn away from that hell once and for all. Deep down I knew only too well what just one more 'fix' would lead to. But it was far from easy and I remember falling into an exhausted sleep afterwards.

It's now that I believe . . . and I want to shout it to the roof tops. God has done it. I am free.

Our holiday in Penang came at the end of those months from the autumn of 1980 through to 1981. There, I was free to love, and was aware that, knowing myself a little, a combination of frailties and strengths, was bringing *me* to our relationship at last.

Upon our return to the drizzle of England that spring we were drawn to the country. If our love was going to flourish, we felt we had to choose the right soil for it and let it take root! Mike found a village house in rural Hampshire, high up on the downs. Born and reared in Dorset, for me, the pull to be in the country was very strong, and circumstances necessitated our making a decision one way or another, quickly. I was three months pregnant by the time I first saw this house, and feeling very sick. With buyers who were pleased with out London house, we sold and bought on the same day.

So we came from that long, wet, but happy spring, to a garden full of deep red peonies and green, neatly edged lawns. Lucinda and Katie's laughter rang out as they learnt to play hide and seek around the trees and shrubs.

Here I would not only forget, but apply my new life and put in the place of negative memories, something enduring – a new future . . . carrying a baby who had been conceived of love, on our holiday, without the help of drugs.

When the sun began to shine, it was like a welcome. We had come home.

Chapter 8

Back to the soil

Being in the country seemed to make us more of a family. At last there was room to sprawl on a real lawn and a chance to drink in the beauty and timelessness of the countryside around us. No longer depressed, I found that such tranquility gently encouraged me to come fully back to life.

After that dismal spring, once the sun shone, we basked in its warmth, eating in the garden and taking picnics into the fields. It was walking on the downs, that expanse of sky over incredible views, and the vegetable garden which featured largest in our lives that summer.

From the day we moved in the vegetable garden had a special place in my heart. Its profusion of broad beans, spinach and raspberries left by the previous owners, flattered my horticultural ignorance. I evolved a habit of disappearing with my hose to think. As I ruminated, the spinach, beans and beetroot got watered, and grew and grew again. It was wonderful!

For me the earthiness of being next to the soil and the cycle of nature went with being pregnant. Sensing that peacefulness that I felt among the vegetables, the children would come down with me and potter. Sometimes they had a competition to see who could fire their broad beans the furthest as they podded them! Mike was clearly staggered by the change in me . . . from hectic rushing around, I was now delighting in the slow pace of life, my enlarging girth and the beauty of the garden. I was thrilled to be alive, wear dirty wellies and breathe the fresh air in that peaceful green place.

On September 10th that year I packed the car up to the roof with tricycles, sit-on tractors and potties. We were ready for our last stay in Dorset with my parents before the arrival of the baby.

Katie was in her cot having a rest before the journey, so Lucinda and I wandered down the garden to pick some flowers for Grannie. She set about her task with gusto, picking all kinds of weeds. I got the hose and dragged it through the beech hedge to reach the remaining vegetables that were looking parched. We must have been down there three quarters of an hour when I felt a sharp pain in my right side, about where my appendix scar sits. I shifted my weight onto the left leg and the stab of pain stopped. 'I'll finish this row,' I promised myself and called to Lucinda, 'Are you ready to go now darling?' She had amassed a huge pile of greenery to take with us!

Then the pain came again and it did not go immediately. Changing positions did nothing to alleviate it. I dropped the hose to the ground beside the raspberry cage and watched the water pool around my feet. Then I started walking carefully with one hand under the base of my stomach. I felt certain it was only round-ligament spasm, and would soon pass. I had had it during other pregnancies but never before at such a late stage.

Through the gate, while I was looking round to see whether Lucinda had decided to follow, I was overcome by the most astonishing degree of pain – much worse because it continued, perhaps for forty-five seconds and made me completely breathless. Will-power and a good sense of balance kept me upright, but I knew the pain was building. I stumbled another twenty feet and collapsed. Moments later, Lucinda, wide-eyed at finding mummy in such an unusual pose, sat on her heels clutching her miniature watering can. Her grin turned to confusion and I tried to reassure her. But I could only say a word or two . . . the pain came again – so strong I had to writhe around, coming to rest on my left side, in a curled heap. Eventually it subsided. This wasn't round-ligament spasm!

We had engaged Hilary, a new nanny, a week previously. I could hear the noise as she vacuumed the car interior, and knew that she would never hear me. So, concentrating on my breathing, I said, 'Lucinda, Mummy is not very well – go and tell Hilly'. Her expression said that she did understand but could not think of leaving me at such a time. As she put a hand on my arm, another pain started to build – it was unmistakeably like a contraction, yet it seemed to make everything in my body scream in agony. So that it was impossible to tell which was the central point of the pain . . . only that it issued from my right side.

I huffed and puffed and could not talk at all. When it was over I just lay there waiting for my breath to come back again. In exasperation, I watched as Lucinda picked the delicate white and pink petals from a daisy, then I reached out to hold her hand.

'Get Hilary. Get Hilary, Lucinda. Get her quickly!' and an involuntary groan emitted from my chest. A tear of helplessness rolled down my cheek. 'Mummy cry', said Lucinda, and then, giving me a last look, she ran up towards the house, pointing at me long before she had attracted Hilary's attention.

I was working out how many weeks pregnant I was.

And I did not need anyone to tell me that this was not a good time to go into labour.

Hilary rang the doctor, who ought not to have been in the surgery at that time, but amazingly she had popped in to fetch something and was able to come straight out to me. Later, I was to appreciate this as an indication of God's control in the situation. She was direct, completely unemotional and gave me some pethidine which brought great relief. Her visit calmed me no end. I sat up and eventually walked to the house to await the ambulance for which she had telephoned.

More myself once again, though still shocked, I had stopped jumping to conclusions and lay on the old sofa in the dining room to dictate some phone numbers to Hilary. We went through a few menus for the girls too. Hilary rang my mother to explain why we were not on our way to stay and the ambulance drew up outside in the drive.

Preoccupied with fear for the baby inside me, I got in, carefully, sad not to have seen Kate. I waved goodbye to Lucinda as the ambulance turned out of our gates, making for Basingstoke District Hospital.

In the labour ward, they monitored the foetal heartbeat, which was fine. So I was told to let someone know when I had another pain. During the entire afternoon there were only two, one of which occurred when the consultant was examining me. As they definitely weren't contractions I began to unwind and stop diagnosing my own condition!

At about 7 pm I was wheeled round to a ward and told that although I had a lot of amniotic fluid there seemed not to be any cause for concern. If the pain did not recur I'd be allowed out in the morning. Because I was an unexpected patient no supper had been ordered for me so I went to bed, disgruntled and hungry.

I slept till about eleven o'clock and woke during a different kind of pain, which went as soon as it came. I turned over and held my breath. What was happening to me? I wondered.

I pulled the sheet up higher and as another pain started, I bit the sheet as hard as I could. There was no mistaking this, it was in my back. 'I have got to get home. I must. I have to,' I told myself. 'Mind over matter. I am not in pain, I am in an anxiety state. Relax and you'll feel fine, girl!' I let all the muscles in the lower half of my body go. But they tightened again within seconds.

This went on for thirty-five minutes, I can remember because I lay there timing it . . . believing fervently that I would go home at all costs.

Then the pain became so excruciating, it made me feel sick and I had to push my buzzer. A staff nurse came and I sobbed out more about wanting to be at home with my family than about my back . . . but I could not hide the waves of stabbing pains that kept sweeping through me.

They gave me more pethidine and I slept fitfully until 6 am – it was raining, driving rain. But it made no difference to me. I knew I should not be going anywhere.

Mike did not go to work, and rang me from the breakfast table. He called again at lunchtime and to ask if I wanted the children brought in, which sounded a nice idea but I had to say no, because I was afraid it would up set them to see me in such pain. So Mike came alone.

I tried to be cheerful. But I knew how lonely the house always seemed to him when I was not there, and the smell of the hospital did not help! We made uneasy conversation. I explained that the doctors were playing some kind of waiting game, and then just as he was talking about getting back to help Hilary finish off the day, I was doubled up with another dreadful pain. When the nurse told him that I was due for another injection but could not have it for fifty minutes I was relieved for him that he had an excuse to go home and wipe sticky hands and faces!

I watched Mike leave my bedside, and listened to his footsteps as they grew indistinct. He was low and so was I. I had not summoned any optimism and was far off remembering telephone numbers and organising menus as I had done twenty six hours ago. Today, I had told Mike to ask Hilary to manage as best she could.

During the first few days, the respite that came between the pains was spent mulling over whether or not I could prevent them being so acute. When the pains actually started I tried to hang on until they stopped. Beyond my immediate vicinity I had no awareness, no interest at all.

It went on like this for about seven days. The only variation being in my mood – one minute I felt okay and then the next very, very frightened. I consumed quantities of Milpar, Colofac and bran until they eventually took effect! I relied on the buscopan or pethidine injections with which I was pumped four hourly round the clock. The injections alleviated the monotony of each day, because immediately after one although I was still very short of breath I felt fine. I would take a constitutional along the polished wide passage to the pay phone and ring home or to Nicola a long-standing friend. Then I would sleep while I could. But in that fourth hour I always promised myself it would be easier. Psyching myself up as best I knew how, I'd lie there in tears thinking, 'How on earth do people get through terrible illness?' and again, 'Keep calm, it won't hurt so much.' But it did. Our ward was modern, light and airy and, thanks to the lovely, chatty cleaning ladies and the other three pregnant girls the week dragged a lot less than it might have done.

By the end of that first week the really terrible moments

were considerably fewer and I was progressing to injections in the evening and codis cocktails when I felt strong and fresh in the mornings. I could not concentrate enough to read, but I was eating light meals. I felt fragile and moved like a tank whenever I ventured out of bed – I was about thirty-four weeks pregnant and I looked as if I was about to have triplets!

As much to help eliminate possibilities as to arrive at a solution, the consultant finally arranged for me to have an X-ray. Everything showed up as expected, and the next afternoon I went down for a scan. Having these tests combined with a falling off in the acute pains convinced me that I must soon be going home. Despite the breathlessness I wallowed in a bath and was shuffling back to my bedside from the bathroom, when I heard the consultant and a doctor come up to the nurses' station. They wanted me to go down for a second scan. I went without giving it another thought.

In the ultra-sound room it was hopeless my attempting to lie on my back, I became completely claustrophobic and panicked within seconds, so they settled for my lying half on one side and then rolling over onto the other. No one spoke much. I could not see the screen properly but I was aware that the consultant was indicating something to the doctor. The machine operator was equally involved.

Then the consultant switched the machine off and very gently sat me up-right, asking if I felt all right. I didn't answer because he continued talking, quietly and deliberately.

'I brought you down here for another scan because it was noticeable when you were scanned this afternoon that there was something behind the baby's neck. It looks to me as though it is about here,' he said, pointing to midway between the tops of the baby's shoulders, at the base of its neck. 'Now that I have seen it myself, I would like to explain certain things to you.'

'I didn't see anything odd,' I said.

'Lie down again then, just for one moment, and I'll show you what I mean.'

He passed the scanning lens over my stomach one last time until he had located the exact spot he wanted, then he pointed to the area of the screen which illustrated the abnormality.

Irritated by my own stupidity, try as I might, I could not see what he meant! I have never been able to recognise more than heads and limbs on those machines. I think, more than that, on this occasion I was already slightly paralysed by its similarity to what had happened with my first pregnancy.

'This can't be happening . . . not again . . . this is unreal,' I managed to say before tears started to well up.

'It looks as though the lump is on a pedicle, which means that it is likely to be operable,' said the consultant. 'What we need to do is to get you to a machine which gives a clearer picture, then we can assess the nature of the lump and the likelihood of effective surgery. We shall take you to King's College Hospital in London where you will be scanned by a friend of mine who has a lot of experience in this field.'

He went off to ring up and try to arrange an appointment for me, and by the time I was back in the ward he was already waiting for me with the news that his friend would be able to see me the following afternoon.

'Now I want you to feel positive about this, Lissa,' he went on, 'because I remember a child who was born here with something like your baby's lump, and she went to Southampton, where surgery has been successful. So get a good night's sleep for now, and we'll know more tomorrow.'

I lay back on the bed staring at the evening sky through the two big windows at the far end of the room. I stuck with my thoughts for an hour or more, then I could not keep it to myself any longer. Whenever there was a turmoil inside me, it seemed second nature to defer to Joanna. 'I'll ring her now,' I thought.

When Joanna picked up the receiver I hardly drew breath until I had blurted out everything. '. . . But I don't feel I ought to tell Mike until after tomorrow's scans. He's had it up to his neck,' I concluded. She was silent . . . it was one of her strengths, to be silent and to wait until she had something to say.

She replied, with quite a bounce in her voice, 'I think you must tell him, you know. It's his baby too and he'll feel really hurt if you don't share this with him. Come on, Lissa!' I didn't need much persuading, but I explained that Mike could not come back that night, so Joanna said she would ring Nicola who was going to see him and we both knew would be the best possible person to break the news gently. Joanna also promised to come to King's Cross Hospital the next day to be with me. What an incredible friend she was!

When Mike rang me an hour later I filled him in as far as I could on what was happening. He was steady and reassuring, but when we said goodbye I felt anything but brave. My mind kept imagining frightening pictures of babies with tubes and oxygen masks . . . my brain already tangling with how long I'd be able to cope with one baby fighting for its life in Southampton and two more at home. However, God gave me complete peace about Mike, and I later discovered that he had been surrounded by understanding Christian friends all evening.

When, eventually, sleep enveloped me that night the shock dispersed as I went under, deeper than I had been in months. As the cup and saucer were put down on my locker and the words, 'Cup of tea for you, love,' reverberated in my waking head, I knew it already! An astonishing change in my attitude had been accomplished. The sense of fear and revulsion at my own baby which had been paralysing me before I slept, were now replaced with love for the child. This morning I was thinking of the baby's soft skin, the little arms and legs, and the face I longed to look into. I heaved myself up so I could sit up in bed and drink the tea. I wanted to *be* with her: 'Little one – I'm ready to do whatever they tell me now, for you. I shall will you to live. Just sleep peacefully and everything will be all right'. I loved that baby with my whole being as we lay there without moving for the hour until breakfast came. I thanked God for the newness of this life inside me and prayed only that I should continue to know that He was with me, by whatever way He chose to reveal his presence.

At King's the doctor, who had come with me in the ambulance went off to announce our arrival. Joanna was already there, so I sat beside her and we talked. She had brought some photographs of our two families taken on a picnic on Watership Down earlier that summer. There was a picture of Katie sitting on a pottie amidst a carpet of grass crowned with buttercups, and the one of us all eating enormous corns on the cob made me laugh. It had been a glorious sunny day, and evoking the memory was a successful diversion.

At Dr Murray's suggestion, we three ate lunch in the canteen, a panelled dining roon packed out with student doctors and nurses. She seemed very subdued, but I was enjoying Joanna's company.

We got upstairs in time for me to change into a hospital gown, then everything and everyone was ready for the off at exactly two o'clock as promised. Several other people crowded into the small room and I was helped on to a bed, which was then tilted back.

The two men, my consultant's friend and the one operating the scanning machine, were working on me for about half an hour. They were working fast out of habit. They must always have needed to, under pressure. It seemed as though there were a lot of details to record too, and presumably they felt, quite rightly, that I wouldn't be able to stand it for very long. As it was I had to shallow-breathe in a succession of quick pants in order to be able to lie down at all.

After a while from the awkward position in which I lay, I looked back to see Joanna and Dr Murray. Each face in the room was glued to the screen, but Joanna smiled.

Then they sat me up for five minutes while a second machine was wheeled into position, and I was asked to lie on my back, this time with my head and chest tilted down. I was by now getting desperate to hear the result, running out of self-induced diversions such as contrasting the characters of the two men working the machines! I saw it as my job to keep myself from fainting, and so concentrated on my breathing, panting like a dog in the hot summer sun. They were measuring the width of the lump, its density, the relation of the growth to other parts of the baby's body. I was told that it was under the baby's chin, not behind the neck as we had thought.

Then I asked the man in charge to point to the growth for me. I had been lying there for nearly an hour, and knew that I was the only person in the room who could not interpret what we were all looking at. Now I too could see the huge cancerous growth. It was vast. I had mistaken it for the head.

I was really baffled by the similarity between the head and the cancer. In retrospect, I think I was protected by my confusion. I would not have been able to go on lying there, keeping still with that weight on my chest, robbing me of air, if I had been in full possession of the facts.

I was wheeled through to another room where a third machine was activated. 'There is only one more thing I need to check,' the man in charge said, 'and then we have finished. It's been quite a marathon for you, I realise that.' I had lost all track of time. It might have been an hour and a half, maybe even two hours since we had started.

He went ahead. It took only another ten minutes or so. He switched something off and turned to look at me, offering me an arm, the shirt rolled up to his elbow. I pulled on it and sat up, searching his expression, then he spoke.

'I could not have been sure without doing this test, but I am now certain . . . there is no chance for your baby. The tumour is of the thyroid gland, and has already begun to eat into the jaw bone. It would seem that, had it not developed this far, the baby would have secondary problems in other parts of the body. If an operation was done, another would soon follow, and then another. There is no hope – I am sorry.'

I did not howl, like I had at hearing about our first child. This one still lived within me. I just cried quietly, and he and Dr Murray left the room . . . they said, to get some tea.

I looked at Joanna, who also had tears in her eyes, and I knew then that I had suspected something like this, all that remained was to stop suppressing the intuitive feeling. My body was already recoiling from the next inevitable step. This time I knew what it would be all about.

'This is unreal, Joanna. Not again . . . it's so awful going through labour knowing you'll have nothing at the end. I'm not sure I can cope this time.' I repeated myself over and over. Then I wiped my nose, straightened the hair combs which were falling out on each side of my head and said, 'It's so late, what about your children? I had no idea we'd be so long. Is anyone organised to pick them up from school? It's nearly half past four!'

'Yes, I'm sure they are okay,' she replied, rather unconvincingly. I decided she was probably sending up arrow prayers for them!

Because I had been asked to spend a final ten minutes on the machine attached to their computer, Joanna said she'd ring Mike at his office. We both knew he would be finding the suspense unbearable.

I went to get some tea, still in a dazed state. I wondered whether I was still me. But as I stood in a narrow corridor looking out, not for the first time, over the tops of London buildings, I thought, this may not be the view from Guy's, but thank God I'm not back 'there' at that stage of my life. This view was equally conducive to thought.

I was staring out, alone and yet not lonely. God was honouring my prayer. It seemed that though the agony almost crushed me I could not blame God. This time I felt acutely aware of His aching with me, and there was a sense of collective reality – actually being a part of the sufferings of mankind.

Before leaving I was monitored for the computer centre, then, exhausted, we returned to our waiting ambulance and Dr Murray sat opposite me as I lay my face towards the upholstery, fighting the tightness in my throat.

The baby kicked and kicked inside me. That had always

encouraged me, but now it only made me long for her to know peace. 'Do you never stop moving because you are trying to get away from that thing which hurts?' I thought, and the flood gates finally burst.

Chapter 9

My rainbow

For some unaccountable reason, on our return journey in the ambulance, I found myself dwelling on two lines from Keats' sonnet 'When I have Fears'. I lay there thinking:

When I have fears that I may cease to be
Before my pen has gleaned my teeming brain . . .

The brain was my mind, as it was, teeming with questions, but the 'pen' was equally relevant. I'd write to Joanna as soon as I had the chance – otherwise she would never know how much her support had meant to me.

Every now and then I put questions to Dr Murray as answers became imperative. The one that bothered me most was finding an explanation for the baby's continual movements. Apart from that hour between my early morning tea and the arrival of breakfast I could not ever remember a time when this baby had been still. 'Do you think the baby is moving because she wants to get away from the lump?' I asked. 'If the cancer is eating into her jaw bone, surely that must hurt? Is the baby in pain?' Tears welled up again. Dr Murray could not give me the answer I wanted: 'I think the baby is aware of pain,' she said '. . . but her appreciation of that feeling is not the same as it would be after birth.'

It had rained during the afternoon. Lying down as we drove, I could see the mixture of colours in the sky. Some white billowy clouds, now lit with sunshine, and others, in the distance, a rich combination of greys, blues and purples, heavy with the rain which was still showering down on north London. Somewhere across the middle of the two was a brilliant rainbow – unashamedly reconciling the weather's moods. God had chosen to mix upon His heavenly palate this very afternoon all the vibrancy and glory of yellows, oranges, reds and blues, and its arc swept the eye upward with it. It was significant . . . I knew.

As the modern buildings of Basingstoke came into view, and I started to focus on the next step, I knew it would be hard to tell Mike about this certain death. Having caught the first available train from Waterloo he was there waiting for us, as the ambulance stopped by the main entrance to the Maternity Wing. The consultant led us into an interview room, the King's report tucked under his arm.

He told us that our baby had an extremely rare cancer – a malignant teratoma – arising in the thyroid gland, and he expressed his own sadness and explained the main points that I had heard in London, which was helpful for Mike, and for me, as I was still trying to take it all in. Then he went on to explain why I must not go full term. The rapid growth of such a tumour might make a Caesarean section inevitable if the baby was not born soon.

There was, however, a danger in stimulating my womb too quickly. 'As this is your fourth labour, it would be unwise to put you under the slightest risk of a haemorrhage, so we won't put up a drip, but we'll take everything very gently. I have no intention of risking your health.'

'How long might it take?' I asked.

'That's impossible to say.'

'Well, at the outside?'

'I don't think we would let you go on longer than three days,' he replied.

I always liked to know where I was. I felt I could last three days, though I would have to pray for that much strength.

We went our different ways. The consultant back to the labour ward, Mike to drive home and make those agonising calls to relations, and me to an unappetising hospital supper. I sat on my bed . . . and waited for bedtime.

In the morning a staff nurse woke me at 6.30 am to give me the first of the induction pessaries. She told me that the doctor would be round to see how I was getting on, and later I was to be moved to a room where I would be alone.

By coffee time, I had only felt one slight pain, so I located my purse and climbed off the bed. 'Blow this for a lark,' I thought. 'If it's going to take forever I need some company!' I went in search of the pay phone trolley and dialled my mother's number. She promised that she and my father would be in to see me after lunch.

Mike sat with me for an hour from one o'clock but when my parents arrived we chatted together only briefly, so he could go home and be with the girls. His weekends had become very precious to them.

My mother must have been shocked when she saw me. Beneath a gaunt face I carried not only the excess water but also quite a big baby. Poor Daddy tried to look relaxed and leaned against the window-sill. We passed a couple of hours in quiet, unhurried conversation, which helped divert my attention from the endless waiting. By bedtime I was having to walk around because the contractions were getting quite painful, but the staff nurse insisted that I go to bed and wait until morning for another pessary. 'A good rest would do you more good than wandering around here getting yourself tired and upset for so little benefit,' she said.

My parents made a second trip on the following day. My father went off for a walk in the grounds but just as my mother and I started to talk freely, Dr Murray breezed in and sat on the edge of the bed. 'Lissa, this is taking too long. It was not our aim to keep you hanging on like this, and though we are right to go slowly it would seem a good idea to take you through to the labour ward now and put up a drip. Because it's possible that when things start moving, it'll all happen quite quickly.'

My mother walked beside me as my bed was pushed out of the room and along the corridor, to the labour ward. Physically large I might have been, but I was very frail at heart. Just having her with me gave me someone to talk to and the audience I needed for the determination not to break down.

When I had put on a hospital gown, the doctor came in and I could smell that dreadful smell that gets up your nose, almost into your forehead and brain. 'I am *not* going to faint,' I stated for the benefit of everyone, including myself. And we all laughed.

When my parents had left I lay there as the second shift of the day went off duty, and the night nurses came on. Surprisingly I did not mind the changeovers too much. With some help from the picture of Lucinda and

Katie propped up beside my bed, this time I was depending more on God.

But the third day was a blur. I had not expected to reach this far without giving birth. Mike came in after breakfast and held my hand for a while, making me feel much stronger. I knew how uneasy he must be feeling, but I begged him to stay as long as he could.

He went out of the room for some time, and I later learnt it was to talk to the consultant. Mike had said that whatever show I was putting across, I was pretty near cracking. It was decided to give me diamorphine and make a plan for speeding things up.

I now felt quite content and drifted in and out of sleep, aware of little more than Mike sitting beside me each time I awoke.

He, on the other hand, was very much aware of the activity and tension which was building around me. It was early evening when I was moved into a delivery room and Mike was persuaded to go out and have a drink and a sausage in a nearby pub. The suspense was interminable. As he turned and left the darkened room, I guessed he was near to tears and my heart went out to him . . . I may be a hopeless patient, but I would rather be in the bed than looking at it!

The unexpected speed which characterised the next phase caught everyone unawares, and Mike was to miss it all. The consultant made the quick snip which was necessary to break the waters, and the next moment his wellington boots slid from beneath him and he found himself flat on his back on the floor! I had to laugh and, to my relief he laughed too. Such slap-stick not only appealed to my sense of humour, but it diffused the intensity of the atmosphere in the room. The waters were still coming, sloshing everywhere. It was like emptying out an entire bath-full. Suddenly I was able to breathe again. Before the consultant left, the anaesthetist was instructed to give me an epidural in case the birth became too difficult. In the event, the epidural had no time to take effect. The baby was born as I rolled on to my back again after the insertion of the catheter. Dr Murray lifted the tiny baby into her arms, 'She is born at last,' was all I could think of.

'We will take her to Special Care till you are ready to see her,' the paediatrician said.

'Thank you but I don't think I do want to see her at all,' I mumbled. I was exhausted now from the weight of the birth and the past fortnight, both of which hung on me like lead.

'You doze for a while,' the doctor said as she left the room with the paediatrician.

I lay on my back feeling drugged. I shivered, drifting in and out of sleep. It was the hospital chaplain's voice which broke the silence around me.

'Would you like us to baptize your baby, Mrs Shortt?' he asked. There was economy of emotion in his voice. 'Golly,' I said. Meaning, in fact, that I felt dreadfully vulnerable . . . how could I take such decisions in this state, on my own without Mike? The nurse went to look down the corridor, but he had not as yet returned.

'We could baptize her in Special Care or in here, whichever you would prefer,' he explained.

'Oh, in Special Care please,' I said.

'What is she to be called?'

'Yes. Yes, do christen her,' I said, my brain taking extra time to assimilate the idea. 'A name. Gosh, I hadn't thought. Is she still alive?'

'Yes, she is. And she is very peaceful,' he said.

'Well, if she was expected to live I know she would have been called Victoria. But that is not right under these circumstances.' I paused to think for a while . . . and he waited, saying nothing. 'To die and be with Jesus . . . she should be called Joy. And as Mike loves the name Cara could we call her that as a middle name . . . I know *Χαρα* means Joy in Greek, but that doesn't matter, does it?'

'Joy Cara it is,' he said and left the room.

Several more dazed minutes passed and then the consultant came in. He walked over to where I was lying and said, 'Sorry I wasn't here. Everything happened so quickly. Has Mike come back yet?' I shook my head, and strangely I felt all right about his not being with me, it meant I could concentrate on what I guessed was about to happen.

'Are you okay?' the consultant asked.

'Sort of,' I said.

'Well, we have talked about this in the past, so you know I think it's important for mothers to see their babies. I've just seen yours, she's lovely, and she will be carefully wrapped in blankets so the lump won't show. Are you ready to meet her if I go and fetch her now?'

'Yes,' I said, and then as I realised how thoughtful he was being I sounded more enthusiastic. 'Yes, please, I'd like that.'

I remember the difficulty I was having in thinking clearly at all. I was trying, though, to say and do what seemed appropriate, hoping that feeling would follow.

I opened my eyes to see them coming in – the tall consultant carrying Joy, a tiny bundle, wrapped in hospital blankets. Her face was quite perfect – her expression peaceful, the head covered in soft dark hair.

I lifted myself on to my elbows to get a better look. 'She

is lovely,' I said, when I felt I had to break the silence somehow. Once it was done, talking came more easily. 'She looks so like Katie did when she was born . . . and yet she is a little like Lucinda. Oh I don't know . . . she is "her" isn't she? And she is beautiful.' I was genuinely touched by her beauty, but each thought came to me as a disjointed part of my experience of her. I could not marshall my thoughts.

'Can I touch her?' I said, needing reassurance.

'You can hold her if you want.'

'I'm so wobbly, I won't.' It was a half truth. I was afraid of whatever it was that the blanket concealed . . . scared the blanket might become unwrapped if she were passed over to me. 'No, I'll just feel her,' I said, surer now.

He lifted her so that she was nearer to me and I could take in each tiny, perfect feature; soft eyebrows, over sleeping lids with their long eyelashes. She was breathing but there was no movement like that which had revealed her torment inside me, no movement at all. She had found peace at last.

First I put just the outside of four fingers on her forehead and then more bravely, with the inside of those fingers and my right thumb, I felt her two cheeks and nose. The skin was warm, alive, but there was not the slightest flinch or evidence of sensation. I studied her face a little longer, hoping to commit it to memory, and then he held her closer to himself again, and I asked, 'Would you mind if . . . well, I would like to pray for her.'

I cannot remember at all what I prayed. It must have included something like, 'Please take her to be whole with you.' But the words were empty for me. I said what I could and inwardly prayed that God would honour my word and take her to Himself, as the Joy she could not be were she to live with me. Then I said goodbye and fell asleep again.

It may have been that the drugs I had had contributed to my muddled thinking and confused the emotional tie which I am certain must have been there. As it was I failed to register then that I would not see her again until the end of my own earthly life. Ultimately, I came to hold her in my mind, feature for feature, from a photograph . . . and began then to appreciate some of the pain I had always suspected she suffered from that grotesque cancer.

My short sleep was fitful and punctuated by nightmares, which terrified me until a sympathetic auxiliary nurse came into the dark room to give me a wash, and take me to a proper bed in a single room.

As the nurse pulled the curtains and began to sort out some of my belongings, Mike put his head round the door. He looked as though he had been rushing. 'It's all over?' he gulped.

'Yes, very quickly. She was born a couple of hours ago . . .'. I paused as the chaplain knocked on the door, and then I finished my train of thought, 'They took her down to Special Care.'

The chaplain came in, and the nurse discreetly left the three of us together, as he spoke quietly.

'I thought you should know. Your baby, Joy, died in Special Care, a few moments ago.'

It was a ridiculous thing to say, but I knew I was going to say it even before I opened my mouth: 'Thank you for telling us.' He told me he would come back when I had had some sleep.

Then I looked at Mike. His head in his hands, he mumbled, 'What was that he said – Joy?'

'Yes, I did not know what to do, darling. You weren't

here and he asked me for her name so she could be baptised. I called her Joy Cara . . . you like Cara, don't you?'

Ignoring my remark he snapped, 'I wasn't here because I was told it wasn't going to happen yet. I've been hanging around for three days, and a fortnight before that, and then I'm not here when it matters!'

'Everyone was surprised that she came so quickly.' I was trying to be conciliatory.

'Don't call her "she",' he grunted. 'I don't want to think of the baby as a person – it'll be easier to forget that way.'

'I shan't forget her, Mike. Not ever. I met her and, despite what I'd feared, she was beautiful.'

That made him cry. With the effect of the drugs wearing off, and aggression mounting between us, the chaplain's words came back to me '. . . you should know that your baby, Joy, has died.'

And I yelled and yelled. It was inevitable that at some stage I would have to let go. I forgot Mike, and could no longer see the dimly lit, small room. The salt in my tears stung my eyes and irritated my cheeks. The agonised, haunting cry went on and on . . . I had had no previous experience of the depth of my soul. I was an open, convulsing chasm – torn apart. As frightened by the noise I was making as I had been of thunder as a child, yet I could not reach the bottom of my grief. The sound of my desolation echoed in my memory for weeks afterwards. Such despair is inexpressible.

As Mike was lifted out of his own dead end of disappointment and loss, he stood beside me. And when he felt that I had tormented myself enough, that there was no point in crying at such a pitch any longer, he lifted my soaking chin and persuaded me to hug him. Eventually the physical contact in the silence spoke to both of us. He helped me down into the bed and stroked back the hair which was falling across my face. Then he left – it was very late.

I can't remember whether I believed at the time that God really does send guardian angels to watch over us in our sleep! But in the morning, after thanking Him for the sunshine which poured into the room, I reached for my *Daily Light.*

I was not interested in the Bible verses for that particular day, but I fumbled through until I found the double page, Morning and Evening, for 21st September, Joy's birth and death day.

And to my astonishment I read:

> We know that all things work together for good to them that love God . . .
>
> All things are yours; whether . . . the world, or life, or death . . . all are yours and ye are Christ's . . . we faint not; but though our outward man perish, yet the inward man is renewed day by day. For our light affliction . . . worketh for us a far more exceeding and eternal weight of glory.
>
> My breathren, count it all joy . . . knowing . . . that the trying of your faith worketh patience. But let patience have her perfect work, that ye may be perfect and entire wanting nothing.
>
> I will pray the Father and He shall give you another Comforter that he may abide with you forever . . . we know not what we should pray for as we ought: but the Spirit itself maketh intercession for us with groanings which can not be uttered.

I read it through twice and then pondered each

sentence 'Wow!' I thought. I lay back on the untidy pillows. Jesus was in that hospital room with me; I let the tears of that discovery roll down my cheeks.

The nurse who came in, whom I don't remember seeing before or since, sat on my bed and smiled. I handed her the open pages, and she read them, and put a hand over mine.

'You are a Christian?' she asked quietly. She had clearly been touched as I had by the appropriateness of these verses. I blinked hard and nodded my 'yes'.

'Praise the Lord', she said, giving my hand a gentle squeeze. It was the first time that phrase hadn't jarred as it was spoken.

The word joy, the name Joy, played on my mind. There was no doubt that I had in some way felt compelled to call her Joy . . . a special name that I would not have expected to choose. The feelings of sadness and hope mingled together. If my intuition was correct that it was Joy's death which had released real joy into my soul, the whole idea was obnoxious unless I understood it in terms of reaching the end of my own resources. I was beat. And beat, God could get close to me. How He planned to do it I was not sure, but I held that little book over my heart, repeating, 'We know that all things work together for good to them that love God.' His presence was like plentiful water in a desert.

I had no need to plunge into self-indulgence. Grief, yes, but there was a hope. Like the sunshine lighting that rainbow. And God had given me a Comforter . . . whose prayer for me had begun within that wailing of hurt the night before.

Chapter 10

An Island . . . surrounded

I spent only a few more days in hospital. When Mike drove me home I felt different and everything looked different. As I got out of the car, still a bit tender, I smelled the air and looked all around me, taking notice of each variety of leaf shape, the flowers and shrubs, I looked further away, across the grass, to the place where I had fallen – where it had all started. It seemed an age ago. I felt thankful that although I was battered, this time I still felt 'me'. And there were the children; I was excited about seeing them again.

I walked gingerly down the step into the kitchen. A spray of flowers that someone had sent me lay on the table. I listlessly plonked them into a tall, white jug, but before I could fill it with cold water, Mike came up behind me and said, 'Oh, come on, you're not going to do anything else tonight. Come and sit down in the study.' He guided me through the hall. 'I wasn't going to do anything else . . .' I said, 'but I feel sort of useless.'

'Don't dwell on things tonight, Twink, it's very early days. I'll go and find Hilary,' he said.

When Hilary and Mike came in and each of them sat

down, I could sense the tension in her body . . . and I shyly opened my arms. She came over to me and we embraced and then she sat down again, this time sinking deep into the seat of the old arm chair.

'Thank you, Hilary, for all you've done, keeping everything going, and making the children happy.' As I spoke I found I was crying at the same time. There were words that I somehow had to get out into the open, across my lips: 'Isn't it awful me coming home with no baby?'

We sat for a moment's awkward pause. It was no use, they would have to grow accustomed to my permanently 'leaking tap'. My grief was characterised by sudden swings of mood, especially in those first four or five weeks. I could switch from touching the heart-ache and releasing some of the hurt, to being quite positive and rational in my thinking, and this all in a matter of seconds.

I wanted to know all about the children and I listened intently as Hilary told us how kind everyone had been. They had been out to lunch and tea several times. I heard lots of different names which my mind failed to register, but my overall impression was that both Lucinda and Kate had found a few friends, and Hilary had enjoyed meeting other families. I did feel for the girls, because having moved to Hampshire so recently, it would have been easier for them to cope in such a crisis if they had had a few familiar faces around. But they were well and this chatter had helped me prepare myself for getting onto the children's level in the morning.

The night passed. I awoke to hear bird song outside the windows and Mike left to catch his usual train at 7.15 am. From my bed I could hear Hilary dressing the children in their room across the landing. I sat up and puffed up my pillows so I could lean back and read some of the many letters which had arrived the day before.

I was really nervous about seeing the children! My heart pounded as I heard, 'Come here a minute Lucinda – let's put a bow on your slide this morning as Mummy's back. No Katie . . . wait for us . . . Mummy has got a sore tummy. You'll have to be careful. There, now you are both ready.' It felt like the start of an exam! I hurriedly combed my hair and straightened the top sheet.

And, at last, they appeared in the doorway, Hilary behind them, a hand in the middle of each back, encouraging them forward. Lucinda paused momentarily and then, with open arms, she rushed across the room to me. We hugged, and then she looked long and hard at me, to be sure I was real . . .

'Lovely Mummy,' she said. I could have cried there and then, but didn't, I felt wonderful, and watched her run over to a pile of toys and books Hilary had sensibly put in the far corner of the bedroom.

Katie had advanced three or four steps during this exchange of affection, but she now stood, looking very serious, saying nothing. Hilary came up behind her and coaxed her gently, 'Go and give Mummy a kiss, Kate. It's Mummy – look she's come back!' But Katie did not move.

If I had thought of adding up what had happened to Kate over the previous few months, I would have leapt out of bed, stitches, tender stomach and all. Sadly I was not wise enough. Mummy and Daddy had disappeared for a seventeen day holiday to the Far East, then we had moved house. A month later Kate had a change of nanny and only days after that Mummy deserted her again for two weeks – this time without even saying goodbye. It was too much for this sensitive twenty-month-old person. She gave me a second or two's glance and then walked, with her customary waddle, to join Lucinda.

It was not until halfway through breakfast, that Kate got up from the rug spread out over the carpet and came over to yank my head down for a kiss. That was all I got . . . but she had broken the ice. It happened later on at bedtime, when Mike was choosing a story to read to them, that Kate let it all out. She suddenly started screaming, caught up in a wild fury of protest. Anger at me for deserting her, anger that there was no baby, anger at herself – why can't I adjust like my big sister seems to have done? – and full circle, to anger and shock at me again.

I felt relieved for her, that at last the emotion had broken. Yet I felt embarrassed too. She had in effect expressed our corporate pain and loss. Had made an outward expression of the family's grief . . . I wondered what would happen among more primitive, less socially conditioned people under such circumstances.

Life was busy during the daytime. Lucinda and Kate always demanding, now craved extra reassurance . . . and Kate suffered understandable anxiety that I was about to do another 'bunk'. I needed to rest between activities, so we played games and drew pictures in my bedroom, and when I got tired, Hilary would lift one child onto each knee and read them stories. Her willingness and gift of merging into the background, quietly getting on with the laundry and cooking until I needed help, was astounding. Remarkably, I never had to ask . . . she just knew, and came at exactly the right moment. I loved her dearly.

Consequently, there was not time for grief when the children were around. They were God's provision for happy times each day; no morning and afternoon were the same and the girls bubbled over with excitement. Their presence I treasured.

I was equally aware of the things which dragged me down. The more I got in touch with previously unacknowledged grief for our first baby, the more acute these experiences became. I would look at Katie and Lucinda as they sat watching 'Playschool' from the foot of our bed, my mind envisaging what it would now be like to have Joy Cara with us. Lucinda would find it difficult to hold her, Katie almost impossible! I went on imagining, seeing it all happening before my eyes, until I remembered another girl, several inches taller than Lucinda, and I visualised a line of four children . . . 'Two of my children are with me,' I thought.

The children, whilst highlighting my loss, were a blessing. Lucinda's spontaneity was particularly helpful in enabling me to do something I found to be essential in coming to terms with Joy's death. Several times she interrupted what she was doing, or something I was involved with, to ask me things about Joy. On the way back from a party, as we travelled along a lonely country lane in the dark, she asked me, 'Do you still cry about Joy, Mummy?'

'Yes,' I said.

'It's very sad isn't it, Mummy, that we have not got a photograph of her. Why didn't you take a photograph, Mummy? Kate and me would have liked that because we didn't see her, did we?'

It was too much. I slowed to a halt and cried my heart out. Lucinda cried with me. And then we shared her hanky and resumed our chatter about the party. It was like that – laugh a little . . . cry a little . . . the only way.

I had been warned to look after my health, and I was trying to eat well, and rest enough, but, as I saw it, undoubtedly the major concern was to get life ticking over normally for the children, and for Mike and myself. Had we still been in London, I probably would have gone shopping with a special friend of mine, Carole, and we would have had cosy suppers with her and her husband, and gone to lunch with Joanna and her two children. As it was, I had no old friends in the area and found going out extremely difficult to handle. Despite my determination to make new friends I could not be jolly and carry on as though nothing had happened. Some how it felt dishonouring to Joy: it was a time of isolation, when I felt that many of the people I ran into simply could not understand how I was feeling.

But the letters which we received penetrated 'my island'. I allowed their words to go deep into my inner self. Because I put up no barriers to them, they effected a variety of totally different but necessary healings.

Carole, who I missed dreadfully, wrote me a fantastic letter, which I have kept. It was so full of the understanding that comes from real perception. Everything in it answered questions I was hardly aware of asking and confirmed other ideas I had had, and she sent me three pairs of jokey socks to buck me up! Her sensitivity was the result of learning to cope after the death of her first baby.

I did try to open up to the people around me, but it was an uphill struggle, and it was always the unexpected which I could not cope with: the bill for Joy's coffin being pushed through the letter box on a Saturday morning when I had just been singing and praising God because I felt so much better. I read the invoice, the minute dimensions of her 'ermine-lined' box . . . and gazed out onto the lawn where Mike was raking up autumn leaves, the girls giggling and trying to help. 'Leave me alone', was my instinctive response as I bit my lip and ran upstairs to fling myself on Katie's bed.

There was an evening at a party, three weeks after leaving hospital when I had a shock, for which I was totally unprepared.

I went upstairs to 'powder my nose' and stick some gloss on my lips and, in search of a mirror, I came across a Moses basket in my host's dressing room. I froze in the doorway. I had not even guessed at what I'd feel if this happened. I looked round to check that no one was watching me and then I crept over to have a look at the contents. It was the tiniest baby . . . maybe a week older than Joy, if that. I found I was daring myself to touch the child. And in time, I could not say how long, I did feel that baby's warm face. It was real, sleeping . . . alive. I crept out again and shut the door so the baby would not be woken by the sound of my sobbing . . . and it was not until the following morning that I realised what a hurdle I had negotiated.

Then there was also my withdrawal from my own husband . . . my own flesh. We suffered separately for quite a long time. This was mainly because of entirely different levels of acceptance of Joy's death. I wondered how Mike could be comforted, refusing, as he did, fully to acknowledge her life; how could I help him to feel that her life had not ended but was gloriously now begun in Heaven? It was as I remembered the first time, a lot easier to talk to close friends about Joy than it was to mention her to her father. Yet for a time, this gap between us served a useful purpose. We found, time and again, that when one of us was down, the other could pull us up . . . so we each had our turn at feeling caring and helpful.

Then one evening towards the end of October, I felt morose and angry that we could not share this deep part of me. I had begun to feel very strongly indeed that God wanted to hold us in His hand, to envelop us and lead us on with a message of hope. It was not right that Mike had shut out the corresponding depth of feeling in his own soul. And I was wanting him. It had begun earlier in the evening when we had talked about the invitation to stay for a weekend with Nicola and James which had arrived that morning. I had said that I wished Mike had a friend like Nicola was to me. 'Someone you could have poured all this out to.' In his reply I had detected a tone of real depression. He had got to the point where he too needed to communicate about it.

We started arguing in the bathroom after supper. I think I eventually climbed into bed and switched the light off, in an attempt to end the day! But it was not much use because I was bursting with pent-up energy and an animated discussion continued until way past midnight. The argument was about something quite trivial, but suddenly we became so verbally aggressive I burst out laughing and said 'This is more like it . . . trying to out-talk each other. Do you realise we are being frank, and actually listening to each other!'

'I know,' Mike said.

'I've been longing for this . . . we haven't *talked*, not like this since . . .'

'And I have missed you . . .' he said. 'Come to me now.'

As words became superfluous, aggression broke the alienation, tenderness said sorry for human fallibility, and we made love in a storm of emotion reaching down into our mutual grief.

Night-time was the hardest, alone with my thoughts. Mike slept quite well during those months. He sometimes said that he hadn't! But I lay awake, for long periods at a time, and his breathing remained monotonously even. Rushing around during the day, I started to bleed badly again and was confined to bed for a month, which was a severe blow. I slept very badly indeed at that time.

There was one particular night when I had gone downstairs at half past one to make myself a cup of tea. Back in bed I just went on staring into the darkness, propped up against the pillows. I was quite peaceful but still very far from sleepy. I looked around me at the familiar objects in the room.

'What place do my raw feelings have in this world of "things"?' I asked myself. 'Lord, you are holding me close to you. Please go on supporting me, and all the other people in the world who suffer, far more than me. Can they know that you care? What in fact makes the difference, believing in you? I must work that one out, because people will ask me. One minute the tangible world around me is so real I feel that I can't get away from it. Then when I confront the pain of remembering my baby, its intensity crowds everything else out. Oh help me!' I finally whispered. Self-indulgence had been building up all day. I now felt utterly miserable and I thought I had no one to turn to. And hours of the dark night stretched ahead of me.

I sensed that Jesus was with me in the room, but I could not bear the fact that I could not touch Him, . . . nor could I handle my baby. Everything in me craved that. It must have been an hour or more of dwelling on my aloneness and my loss before I struggled deeper into my subconscious, realising that I was grieving the first baby's death too. 'Why had I not insisted that she be given a name, and a burial?', and a moment later I was accusing myself of not feeling the loss of her, which must have hurt her? 'You were only half a person' I scolded.

The accusations came thick and fast. 'Why did I not hold Joy? She only lived for two hours . . . and she spent that time . . . *all by herself!'* For all that time, her only time, when I could have been giving to her, I did not. All I plucked up the courage to do was to touch her . . . 'Pitiful . . . how can you live with yourself?' I thought. It was brutal.

I had allowed her to die alone – she had not felt my arms around her. I felt sure I would never recover from such guilt.

Then my mind filled with doubts about the consultant's words . . . did she really have to die? Could they have operated? Why, oh why, did she have to die anyway? 'Lord can you hear me . . . I can't stand it, do you hear me!' The tears were flowing down my cheeks, I was in hell. I was cut off from everyone and everything . . . consumed with sorrow.

I thought and thought. Going inside, outside, round about, and then unravelling it all again. Perhaps two hours passed before the first glimmer came as I was reliving the feeling in my fingers as I touched Joy's face – it had happened five weeks earlier. 'She did not move. Did she?' I remembered. 'She had no reaction' I said aloud, softly, but with emphasis. I let it sink in. 'That is amazing, thank you Father' I thought. I shut my eyes tightly, to allow that thought to spread through my body . . . it was gradually spreading like an ointment for healing. 'Even if I had held her she probably would not have been aware of me.' It was like a reprieve.

Then, when He had come into the thought process, as it were, I became aware of Jesus. God the Father was like me . . . in that He understood better than anyone my agony. He had sent His only Son to die . . . I had lost two daughters, but I also had two daughters. His Son had died . . . not like Joy, and countless others in this fallen world . . . He who was perfect had died – for me. I had caused His death. And because of that very death I was now able to come close to God, to come through in my thinking, to God. He was hearing me. None of the Easter Story had ever struck me like this before. It was as if God was saying, 'It's okay, it's okay, I know . . . I lost my *only* Son . . . I didn't have another like you do!'

I lay there, crying intermittently each time I thought of Joy, and as I appreciated that *God* Himself had touched my heart. When dawn faintly lit the curtains, my thinking had brought me as far as acknowledging that death was not an end. Somehow God had ordered the whole night, releasing into my mind only such thoughts as were appropriate for each hour in time.

While I waited for the alarm to go off I started to thank Him for Lucinda and Kate with such an urgency, as if I had never done so before. This experience had changed me. I was to see life and its infinite possibilities differently, to measure and order my life by different criteria. I had faced fear itself tonight. Now it was my responsibility, having been led away from it, to live free.

While Mike was getting dressed I opened my Bible. And I read, from Isaiah 61, 'The Lord has anointed me to bring good tidings to the afflicted, he has sent me to bind up the brokenhearted, to proclaim liberty to the captives.' That is what He had done for me in those long dark hours. I could hardly believe that God had planned for me to read that, to drive it home, so I would not forget in the future that He had indeed been caring for me, suffering with me during that night.

I read on, enjoying the next few chapters, as I might have done a novel. Until I reached Isaiah 65 and the passage about the new creation:

> Be glad and rejoice forever in what I create. The New Jerusalem I make will be full of joy (*that word again!*) and her people will be happy . . . There will be no weeping there, no calling for help. Babies will no longer die in infancy . . .

God knew – knew only too well how much it hurts to lose a baby. So much so that it is written in His word, written down thousands of years ago!

But what about 'rejoice forever in what I create?' Did God just want me to rejoice in Joy, even though she was no longer with me? Surely there was more to it than that. I had it on my mind about life coming out of death. So I shut my Bible and searched for a letter Joanna had sent a few weeks before. I found it tucked inside a book I had been reading. I began writing to her about the Isaiah 65 verses and how much better I felt for having gone through such a night. Then I read her letter through again. It had been written soon after our visit to King's, specifically to ask me whether I had seen the rainbow in the sky on our way home. But I had not really taken in Psalm 126, which she had quoted at length. I now looked it up – a very short psalm, full of contrasts. 'Those who sow tears shall reap joy.'

I scribbled on to her, 'Have just re-read your letter, and Psalm 126 twice . . . Tell me, do you think that Joy is going to have brought me great joy in time to come?' I did not know what it was to be, but I knew *something* was going to have been born from Joy's death.

I did not go on to rethink my views on certain things, as I knew God wanted me to do. Life was tough going, especially in view of my having to stay in bed for so long. My efforts to resume normal life quickly and so forget the bed-ridden days in hospital all went haywire. So, energetic though I am by nature, with the cherry trees changing colour outside my window, and the woody smell of fires, and ploughing beckoning from the downs, I had to lie still. I could see myself falling into depression but could do nothing about it. The first month had been hard, but by the third month I continued to feel isolated from those around me and found, to my astonishment, that on the beaches of my island there were still signs up: 'No landings, visitors unwelcome'. And I was prey to guilt and self-accusation, even after that special night when I had felt so close to God.

I lost all interest in my appearance, putting on weight, for which I blamed the severe winter and my craving for chocolate . . . I didn't care. Most decisions terrified me. Whether the children should have Marmite or honey on their toast seemed an insuperable problem. My doctor told me to take pressure off myself, and stop trying to do so much, but I was, despite everything, emotionally volatile.

When the ups and downs after Joy's death had evened out a little, I began to have fun writing more than just letters. My mother gave me a typewriter for my birthday in September 1982 and I began to believe that if I did nothing more in my life than write about Jesus' love being real and active, Joy's short life would have been worthwhile. My attitudes began to change.

What I was not prepared for was the nausea which hit me two months later, shortly before Christmas. I tried not to think about it. I thought I had received direct encouragement from God for my writing. I was planning a book . . . this book. But God was intervening . . . to add a new chapter.

Chapter 11

Seven Times Hotter

I was driving wildly! Not at all like a responsible mother should. And I had the children on board too . . . normally I was far more careful.

I glanced in my rear-view mirror; to see their faces. Once we had negotiated the roundabout we were currently approaching, far too fast, I would spring my news on them! On that grey January afternoon the rest of Reading appeared to be getting on with its own business but I was . . . distracted!

'We are going to have a celebration,' I said finally as we drew to a halt for a moment by some traffic lights.

'What's that?' asked Lucinda.

'It could be a peach melba,' I said, purposely missing her point! 'Would you like that?'

'Why is that a cellebating?' Katie asked.

'We're going to do something or have something very nice this afternoon, because we have something to be excited about.' I watched their faces as I spoke.

'What? Tell us!' they said, almost together.

'You'll never guess . . .' I teased, dragging it out. Wanting to remember this moment for a lifetime. I needed their full attention. 'We are going to have two babies. I went to the hospital this morning and I have got two babies growing in my tummy.' They stared at each other . . . astonished! Then a broad smile crept across each little face and Lucinda took a deep breath and said, 'Two babies . . . two babies, Mummy – golly gosh!' 'So we will have one baby each,' Katie instantly worked it out! She turned to Lucinda and informed her, 'You can have one baby and I will have the other.'

'Where does that leave me?' I asked jokingly.

As I parked the car I could not help thinking that it would have been impossible to imagine a better reaction from the girls. They were now bursting full of it.

On our way to the store Katie said to an old gentleman, 'Do you know that my Mummy has got two babies in her tummy?' The man winked at me, disbelieving. I was only twelve weeks pregnant!

I was so determined that someone should celebrate this startling bit of news that I did order each of them an indulgent peach melba, which they almost finished. While I felt ill sipping from a glass of Perrier!

This news, a result of the tiniest, smaller-than-a-pinprick of a hole in my contraceptive diaphragm, had next to be broken to Mike. That night as we were finishing a story upstairs, the playroom door banged, so I agreed it was time to tell Daddy about 'our news'.

We all sat waiting for him. His brief-case was left in the hall, and as soon as he heard the girls' suppressed laughter he came up to see them. The instant his head and shoulders appeared in the stairwell, they cried in unison, 'Daddy, Mummy's going to have babies!'

Plodding on slowly up the flight to the top he said, 'I know.'

Then as he came into the room, lowering his head to avoid the low beam, he must have had a double-take.

'Babies. Bab-*ies!*' he said and looked at me as if longing for me to tell him it wasn't true! 'Yes,' said Lucinda, 'the doctor says Mummy's got two babies in her tummy – and she's got a picture of them . . . look, you can see.' I had shown them the polaroid that the woman working the scanning machine had given me.

It was funny how I had found out about them. Lying there on the slab, petrified that there might, again, be something wrong I had asked, 'You will tell me if you can see anything the slightest bit unusual, won't you? You know I can take it. I've had to before now.' The man immediately turned to me and said, 'Well . . .' and my heart sank.

'It depends whether you think that more than one is abnormal!'

'It might not be for someone else – but as I wasn't expecting any . . . I don't know . . . what do you mean exactly?'

'Mrs Shortt, there is Twin I and . . . wait a minute, yes, here is Twin II. Do you see where I am pointing?' 'What!' I said, 'I don't believe it. At least I do . . . oh, how fantastic!' It was exhilarating!

I did not tell Mike this story that evening – he would not have listened, even if I'd wanted to tell it to him. Instead I just confirmed what the children were saying. 'Yes, we are having twins,' I said, quietly.

'Oh no, oh no, I'm not having anything!' he said, and disappeared through our bedroom door to the bathroom. The girls looked at me, a trifle disappointed, and I said that I thought it must be quite a shock for poor Daddy. Then I tucked them up, and we said 'thank you' for the day, and I tiptoed out of their room.

I heard Mike turn the bath taps off and with determination, I went into the bathroom. He was lying in deep water, the room filling with steam, but the heat made no impression on his 'commuter's pallor'. The dark mornings and even darker nights always turned his skin grey by the end of January; tonight it had taken on a greenish hue.

I put the loo seat down so that I could sit and talk. He said nothing. Neither did I. Then, with all the stage sense of a Shakespearian actor, he spoke: 'You have ruined my life.'

I waited a bit longer, but he did not go on. By the time a hundred thoughts had whizzed through my mind he got round to enlarging on it. 'Now I shall be locked in for life. This house is too small, I shall never be able to give four children what I would like to . . . and have you forgotten how ill you were the last time you were pregnant? I can't go through that again. We have had nothing but disasters having babies, don't you see, I don't want to end up without you, and the girls need you.'

'But, Mike, this may be the way that God can show us that He loves us by giving us two babies in place of the two we lost!'

'After all that's happened, what on earth makes you think that?'

All my barriers were going up fast. 'That's quite a lot for me to be thinking about,' I said. 'I'll go and get the supper while you're dressing.'

As I left the bathroom he grunted, 'I don't want any supper, I feel sick.'

Poor Mike. I knew slightly what he was feeling, but I had no experience of the extra pressure of being a wage earner in a home. I had begun to enjoy having children who played by themselves while we read the papers after Sunday lunch. I had sold my nappies and we were planning to take the girls abroad with us the following year. We knew we could afford two children . . . in a way it was as simple as that. We had, together, acclimatised ourselves to having two, rather than the original dream of four children, shared in those letters between England and Italy eleven years before.

And Mike's concern for my health seemed valid. I was anxious about carrying one, let alone two babies, in a womb that had nurtured such a malignant cancer. But as I laid the supper tray, I could see that there was not a particular worry which bothered him . . . it was far more the relentless battering he had received, ever since the day we got married.

During that first conversation in the bathroom I had felt that these babies were God's present to us. I have no doubt I could have made an adequate 'case for God', but I sensed that Mike didn't want to listen.

As I tried to fall asleep after a late supper, I could not stop mulling over what Mike had brought up . . . What if one or both of the babies had something wrong with them? The panic of that night waiting to go up to King's suffocated me . . . How would I ever cope with the mixed emotions of welcoming one twin into the world, whilst mourning the other?

I remembered what the gynaecologist at Guy's had told me, at my first ante-natal check, when I was pregnant with Lucinda 'You have got to face the fact that either you conduct yourself throughout this pregnancy in fear and trembling, or you adopt a positive attitude, looking after yourself and the baby calmly and with common-sense.' I smiled, thinking now how right he had been – considering my bulimic lifestyle it had been a miracle that I had carried Lucinda even the thirty-five weeks which I managed. Peace of mind about the baby had been a vital part of holding the rest of me together.

So I decided that night that I would do whatever

would most benefit the babies, and just try to live through the next six months until God took His chance to say to us both, and especially to Mike, 'Look, here you are . . . trust me!'

But nothing is that easy! As always, once a chink appeared in the armour of our marriage, the arrows came raining in from all quarters. When my barriers had gone up, so had Mike's. He doubted the wisdom of my going ahead with the pregnancy, and wore a spirit of pessimism which nothing could lift.

The gynaecologist was encouraging and sounded as excited about this wonderful surprise as I was. He set about monitoring and looking after the pregnancy with great care organising plenty of scans, to keep watch on the babies and to keep me happy, and at Mike's insistence he arranged a meeting with the chief geneticist in our area. At our meeting at the hospital I found that the geneticist not only had with him every conceivable piece of relevant information on all four of my previous children, but he had also taken trouble to speak to the doctor who had counselled us at Guy's after the first death. We spent about three quarters of an hour talking about each pregnancy and birth. I found myself gaining confidence because he had not only done his homework, but it had sunk in, and he was sharing the dilemma of my situation from a position of genuine concern. After enumerating the risks as well as the likelihood of one or both babies being normal and healthy, I called Lucinda and Katie in, and he examined their heads with considerable attention to detail.

I left the hospital with my excitement about the pregnancy rekindled. The girls and I leapt down the stairs to the car park two at a time and Lucinda actually said, 'Mummy, you do look happy!' as we sat on the grass verge and hugged together for a moment. I could not have put it into words, but everything was slowly but surely beginning to point in one direction . . . go ahead, love the thought of these babies, and you will be able to love them when they come. I felt marvellous, and relieved about the interview, and it buoyed me up because Mike and I were rubbing each other up the wrong way at home.

In my broody, fulfilled state, receiving excellent hospital reports about the babies' growth, I was guilty of failing to love Mike enough to help him with his fears. I regret it now, but I can only think back to the extraordinarily maternal frame of mind I found myself in, which I seemed unable to transcend.

Getting big so quickly, it became a task of momentous proportion to move around. Later that summer, in June, I would lie on the bed in the afternoons, eagerly anticipating Wimbledon, but usually fell asleep in the first set. Some people write books, run businesses and play tennis until the end of their pregnancies; but not me. I was not even good company! I seemed to be a whale of hormones, motherliness and discomfort. There were children wanting stories read while others got their heads and limbs stuck under my rib-cage. One needed a lap for a cuddle but risked getting kicked at from within. So Mike got left out. Partly because in a way I could not help it, and, as much, because of the sense of rejection I felt at his failure to join with me in the happy anticipation of a complete family.

We had an argument one evening which evolved from Mike's conviction that I did not understand his point of view, and was not even trying to. 'Or you wouldn't take that attitude!' he accused.

'Oh Mike,' I said, 'I've decided to try and do everything

I can to look after these babies, come on – you'd do the same if you were in my position. Why can't you see it like that . . . I think you will one day. Anyway you'll feel quite different when they are born, I'm sure.'

I knew the anger was rising in him. He made a remark about not being around when they were born, and then he flung his supper tray across the floor. I sat there speechless. I know I ought to have stood up and hugged him . . . but I felt so hurt, he was more like an enemy than a partner, and as my vision went blurry I opened the study door and slowly walked up the stairs.

What I wrote when I had grabbed a notepad from my desk in the bedroom is unprintable. All I was aware of was my own unhappiness. I guess Mike, downstairs, was in a similar place. I was so low I spared nothing . . . just writing it all down, every little bit of the selfish despair, the aloneness, that wasted time, which should have been spent together . . . The world was dark.

I read through my scribblings, cried some more and then decided to act. I needed help . . . just to keep me together. So I rang Sally, a friend who lived about half an hour away, and explained, without going into any details, that I needed her advice. Then I asked her. 'Could you pray about whether it's right for you to help. Jane, Gail and I are due to meet together this week so I'll ring them to find out whether they would mind if you joined us.'

The plan dovetailed beautifully and I not only managed to contact the others, but when I rang Sally back a second time she had thought it through to the point that Thursday would be the best day for a number of reasons. It was the *only* day for the rest of us. So that was fixed.

My expectations were high as I parked in Gail's drive

on that Thursday morning. I felt peaceful, prepared for whatever came from the morning and Gail's sixteenth century thatched farmhouse was tranquility itself, the white walls and exposed beams idyllically surrounded by a blanket of fresh green grass and spring growth. The four of us chatted over coffee, comfy chairs were arranged around the huge old fireplace and the atmosphere was welcoming and friendly. We were close, and it seemed natural to be there together – for me to have asked them to have faith for me, and their enthusiasm about coming had been reasurring.

Jane prayed for God's blessing on the morning. Then I said, quietly, 'In one way I feel selfish asking you all to come to put me back together again. In another I don't though . . . because if I end up having a breakdown, I shall be even more a nuisance to everyone. So thank you for coming . . . I haven't got another thing to say . . . I feel terribly empty.'

They took over. I just sat and listened and they talked some more and prayed a little, then Sally, said that she had asked God for a clear word which she could be sure was for me. God had led her to read Daniel Chapter 3. I remember registering surprise that this Old Testament book could be relevant to my carrying twins! But opening my Bible I said nothing – it occurred to me that God could see, from His perspective, what was, deep down, the matter . . . mine was only a superficial understanding.

So we all listened as Sally began reading about Nebuchadnezzar's golden statue on the Plain of Dura – immense it was! – and the people who were told to fall down flat on the ground to worship the statue. 'And anyone who refuses to obey will immediately be thrown into a flaming furnace.' Which was what actually happened to Shadrach, Meshach and Abednego.

I was hearing the story dimly. Such words as 'our God is able to deliver us' could be significant but my situation was hardly like that of God's servants Shadrach, Meshach and Abednego.

As Sally read I sensed that I was being spoken to as she described the furnace. It was heated seven times hotter for those men. But I did not feel the touch of God until she read verse 25:

> ' "Well look!" Nebuchadnezzar shouted. "I see four men, unbound, walking around in the fire, and they aren't even hurt by the flames! And the fourth looks like a god!" '

It all fitted . . . and further down the page were the triumphant words, 'For no other God can do what this one does.' It was addressing me directly. Sally stopped reading at the end of the chapter and said, humbly, 'I had a strong feeling that I should read this to you. I couldn't work out why, expect perhaps because God wants to tell you that however tough things may get – even seven times worse – He is in those situations with you.' She paused and then added, 'He loves you, Lissa.'

I couldn't speak for a moment, but the others waited, sensing that something was wanting to out! 'It's amazing – that God could have led you to that! I hadn't realised but the one fear which has dominated me for the past two months is that one baby might die, or might be born unable to walk or . . . anything. That's what is frightening Mike too . . . on top of his fear that something might happen to me. Don't you see? There were *four* men, able to walk around, and *unhurt*. So nothing is going to go wrong.' I put a hand to my stomach.

'Both the babies and me are going to be okay, all three of us . . . and the fourth person's a god . . . Jesus. That is the most fantastic confirmation of what I first believed before the doubts crept in, that God wants to love Mike and me through these babies.'

We were silent. It was as though God was there in the room with us . . . enabling me to comprehend the significance of the security and peace which this message was going to give me over the coming months. The quiet was broken as prayer became the natural response and the Holy Spirit continued to work in Sally, showing her that I needed direction and something to hold on to, that I could keep with me.

We spent the rest of the time discussing what I should aim for in my relationship with Mike. I agreed that we needed to get back to communicating, and that we should spend more time alone together. The others' enthusiasm infected me and we made plans for my well-being, under four headings, mental, physical, spiritual and practical.

It was gradual, but that very evening, the ice between Mike and me started to melt. On his return from work he parked the car near the back door and crossed the lawn to where I was sitting behind a table with an open Bible on my lap, the tray of drinks ready. It was not yet warm as it would be in June or July but quite pleasant enough to sit outside, though the sun had already disappeared behind the trees. Mike smiled, which in itself said, 'Thank you for the welcome, for having the children in bed and looking as though you want to talk instead of falling asleep!' Because God was there in that evening together, Mike came out from behind his barrier. We talked of that morning, and were forgiving about the previous five months. We shared our fears, and planned a weekend away with the children and some great friends. 'Wow!' I thought, not for the first time, 'God seems almost to delight in impossible situations so that we can see His glory when He acts!'

Despite human inadequacy, God was slowly filtering through to us His vision of our life together.

Five weeks later Gail and I went to a healing service in London which further helped my peace of mind. I asked for healing and cleansing for my womb, and Jesus' continued protection for my babies. I was cut free from certain past ties which had undoubtedly been a block, some of which had been worrying me. Wonderfully I handed over to God my concern for Mike – his depression and fear . . . and experienced a tremendous lifting of the weight of responsibility I had been carrying around with me because of Mike's recent reactions. I found myself expecting God to move in unlikely ways . . . thrilled that He as bigger than I had ever dreamt. Yet He remained personal.

As He did on the weekend spent with Nicola and James in Gloucestershire, when we prayed and talked about the damaging effect of a spirit of pessimism and read from Isaiah 66, ' "Shall I bring to the point of birth and then not deliver?" asks the Lord your God. "No! Never!" ', and then, 'Rejoice with Jerusalem: be glad with her, all you who love her, you who mourned for her.'

I cried when I thought about substituting Mike and me for Jerusalem – Nicola and James had so often mourned with us . . . and loved us, giving to us in so many ways over the years. It was as though God was saying 'I have better for you – be open and receive it.'

As the pregnancy progressed I linked the varied assurances God had given me. They were times when

God had spoken, and as such they were precious beyond words. They were also active. He used them to build up my understanding of unconditional love . . . and I had begun to be myself as I never had done before. For someone who had once been so jittery she could not relax in her own home, I marvelled at being able to sleep and eat and look after myself.

The night before I went into hospital to be induced at thirty-nine weeks, I went with friends to a praise evening. I had no strong feelings about it, but it seemed a good idea to be a part of the body of Christ and to say thank you publicly to the Lord for all He had done to help me through those long weeks. After the singing the Lord said to me through friends that this was the end of our troubles, 'I want to bless you' He said. I know that every one of the thirty or forty people in the room were praying that I would believe those words and take them to my heart.

So I approached my labour with an eager anticipation; determined that I would enjoy the experience as far as possible, on the assumption that numbers five and six could not be too difficult.

Despite the words 'twin regime' written in red ink on the top of my file, I did not have an epidural. I settled down on my own to ride the contractions as best I could. When I reached contraction number seven I huffed and puffed through that painful stretching and then inwardly chuckled and thanked God that He was still close by me, even after the seventh.

It went slowly at first. But eventually the contractions intensified and the midwife agreed that I was ready to move into the delivery room.

Within minutes of my arrival I was pushing for all I was

worth and suddenly a slippery person made his exit on to the end of the bed.

'You have a little boy, Mrs Shortt,' said someone! I looked down at him. 'James – hello little James,' I said. 'Welcome to life.'

We had a brief cuddle and then he was put first onto the scales and then into a cot, not far from me, as I was encouraged to remember that I had to make at least as valiant an effort for Twin II!

I pushed once, and then again. But the obstetrician told me to pause a moment while he made sure what was happening to the baby. The look of dismay and panic in the eyes which stared above the mask would have really got me going if I had not been thinking at that precise moment about the furnace getting hotter. He reached further inside me, and then once his original fear was confirmed his tone of voice changed completely.

'Get her to theatre – *quick*. And fetch the consultant – he must come immediately . . . that baby has been waiting long enough.'

I remember the short journey to theatre. And then being surrounded by people . . . masses of them . . . everywhere. The consultant arrived at once and the anaesthetist told me she would give me an anaesthetic quickly because no one wanted to risk my baby's life. I think the consultant explained a little more . . . and then I was 'gone'! And they were frantic! The second baby was presenting arm first and James's placenta had started to follow him out.

The next thing I knew was waking to an indescribable discomfort in my tummy. I was aware of Mike on one side of me and the consultant on the other.

'Lissa, you have got two boys . . . they are terrific fellows. Twin II had a rather squashed arm, but it looks better already. The little lads are doing very well in

Special Care. Sorry if you feel sore . . . you'll soon get over that.'

'Yeah!' I said, and groaned. But I was already glowing, regardless of the pain, from that incredible news . . . and then I believe I fell asleep again.

As I sat with my cup of tea, exactly one week later, in Dorset, looking out to sea, I relived those moments again and again. Old Harry Rocks and Studland rose out of the water to my right and the sun shone on the Isle of Wight to the left. The girls were already riding their bikes furiously around the patio, the sea breeze whipping their hair around their happy faces.

Mike was standing over the big pram, and in it lay the two little boys, in nappies and long sleeved cotton vests, hip to hip. Mike is not given to poetry, but his expression spoke for him: This is God's love to us. Our family completed in James and William.

The Lord has done great things for us, we are glad.

Postscript

One day I shall face Jesus and ask – Why did it have to be like this? So painful. Even though in my heart of hearts I know. He has wanted to show me that He is everything to me. It is as though, walking through my life, He has looked down on each stone . . . rolled it over, and if, on the underside, there has been dirt, has swept it away Himself.

As I have endeavoured to relate the inner struggle, I have neglected describing my life as others could see it. Some will turn round to ask, 'Was it really that bad?' and 'Surely you have exaggerated!' To which I would reply, 'Go and ask any bulimic or anorectic, who is suffering now, in that hell . . . and talk to the mother who has this morning, visited the grave of her dead child.'

I was once a perpetrator of lies. Today the foundation for this story is its truth. However, unlike other periods in my life – of which I only seem to remember the happy days – while I was depressed, the depression seems to have swallowed the lighter moments into itself.

Yet there were good, genuinely good times, even then. Most of them spent out of doors, in the fresh air. Mike and I have always adored walking. If we were not going to the country at the weekend we would drive to Kingston or Kew or Windsor Great Park, and walk anywhere between three and seven miles, according to the mood. That way we talked, and stayed friends, especially during many dreadful weekends . . . our walks were what made life bearable. They meant too that when the week got on top of us and we each needed something pleasurable to look back on, it was upon that enjoyable part of the previous Saturday or Sunday that our minds focused.

Living so close to the Thames in Fulham, we felt an affinity towards the river. We would walk by it in silence or in heated debate, the pace always brisk. We passed under bridges, by boathouses, couples hand in hand, mothers with toddlers, old men and dogs, and the water flowed on beside us, glistening in the daylight, reflecting the banks and the willows which overhung it.

Then there was a glorious long weekend in the Lake District, visits to Glyndebourne, ski-ing holidays, hot summer holidays, graduation when I collected my degree, enjoying my children and memorable weekends with close friends . . . but through these bright moments ran the thread of bulimia and depression. I had read in the Bible that nothing could separate me from the love of God, but living through crisis after crisis I did not have His perspective on those ten years, I never felt free to fully enjoy these pleasures. More significantly I failed to understand that God was not doing an instant, superficial healing . . . but was working gradually towards a 'complete healing'. As a result, I panicked and despaired more than I ever rested on the promises of God.

The worst years of my eating obsession pushed my

faith into a tight corner, so that my initial love for Jesus, stemming from the night I gave my life to Him, had become diluted. Nevertheless, Mike and I tried, more by rigid discipline than out of desire, to continue going to church. During this time my spiritual anchorage came from Dorset.

We only went down to the West Country every two months, but it became a habit, when we were there, to drive over to Canford Magna, where the Reverend John Collins was Vicar of the Parish Church, and as it were to 'sit at John's feet'. The man never failed to take the opportunity of hammering home that Jesus was Lord over all things. 'He wants to be Lord of *your* life', he'd say.

I would sit there, in my highly nervy state, thinking, *my* Lord? How do *I* get Him up there onto the throne of my life? It is surely impossible to do that if one is labouring under the pretence of a normal life as I am.

The church itself stands surrounded by the grounds of Canford School which are very beautiful, and from the moment I stepped off the gravel path into the porch of the church, I always sensed God's loving presence. The message we heard offered healing and light. Yet I simply did not know how to appropriate them to myself. On two separate occasions, perhaps a year apart, I went up to the altar rail to receive the bread and wine, and tears started to flow from me, till my face and hands and whatever scraps of tissue I could find in my pockets were literally saturated.

The first time this happened the assistant offering me the bread put it down for a moment and laid both hands on my head. Still the tears came, pouring forth until I felt that I had somehow been washed down. On the other occasion, John Collins looked so sympathetic toward my unhappiness I almost said to him, 'Don't worry for me – the Lord Jesus is here with me in this dreadful state'. And, as I went back to my pew I heard what God was trying to say to me: 'You don't have to *do* anything. It is not *you* who will put *me* on any throne! You think people don't understand what you are going through . . . I do. Yes . . . you can cry before me. But just remember, you don't have to do anything. I love you as you are . . . stop striving.'

Writing this down has been both a remarkable and a painful experience for Mike and myself. I had not realised before just how much God had done with us, and until committing it to paper, God had not closed off the hurt. Because it has been since finishing this manuscript that God has given me an assurance of a new start, in the same world but with altered expectations. With God's love there are no limitations, and I have begun to see evidence of real change in my attitudes. I am learning that my relationship with my husband is more important that any other demands on my love and time; that the children's happiness is more important than the way they look; a welcoming home more important than a showcase.

Taking me beyond myself, God has opened me up to Him and to others around me . . . so that this is not an end but a beginning.

> We know that in all things God works for good with those who love him . . . For I am certain that nothing can separate us from his love: neither death nor life, neither angels nor other heavenly rulers or powers,

neither the present nor the future . . . there is nothing in all creation that will ever be able to separate us from the love of God which is ours through . . . Jesus.

Romans 8

If you wish to receive *regular information* about *new books*, please send your name and address to:

London Bible Warehouse
PO Box 123
Basingstoke
Hants RG23 7NL

Name ______________________________

Address ______________________________

____

____

____

I am especially interested in:

- ☐ Biographies
- ☐ Fiction
- ☐ Christian living
- ☐ Issue related books
- ☐ Academic books
- ☐ Bible study aids
- ☐ Children's books
- ☐ Music
- ☐ Other subjects

P.S. If you have ideas for new Christian Books or other products, please write to us too!